HOW TO GET OUT—
IF YOU'RE IN OVER YOUR HEAD

by
Ted Nicholas

First Printing — January, 1976

Library of Congress Number — 75-45878
ISBN — 0-913864-04-8

Published by
ENTERPRISE PUBLISHING COMPANY
1300 Market Street
Wilmington, Delaware 19801

TABLE OF CONTENTS

TABLE OF CONTENTS (cont.)

ACKNOWLEDGMENTS

Individuals who have made valuable contributions to this book include Joseph Hutton, for suggestions on the manuscript and invaluable research; Robert H. Blumberg for helpful suggestions on the subject of bankruptcy; Thomas W. Hutchins, for assistance with important decisions on the format; Sylvan N. Levy, Jr., for encouragement and moral support; and Sara Leigh Krylow for proofreading and typesetting the entire book in a remarkably short time. A good job on the charts was done by Margaret R. Buchanan.

A special acknowledgment belongs to the many hundreds of people in the United States who, within the last two hundred years, have worked toward a more humane approach toward debtors. Included in this list are the framers of the U.S. Constitution, which gave Congress the power to establish laws on bankruptcy, and countless lawyers, judges and laymen who have made contributions toward the elimination of debtors' prisons as well as laws for the orderly handling and disposition of matters arising between debtors and creditors. Their efforts have enabled many honest men and women to overcome debt problems and gain a fresh start, a fundamental necessity in a dynamic free enterprise economic system.

T. N.

LONGWOOD LIBRARY

Longwood College, Farmville, Virginia 23909-1897

A center for learning. A window to the world.

Library hours during regular sessions
Monday-Thursday .. 8 a.m. - 12 midnight
Friday .... 8 a.m. - 9 p.m.
Saturday .... 10 a.m. - 9 p.m.
Sunday .... 1 p.m. - 12 midnight

Overdue fines after August 24, 1998
Books .... $0.25 per day
Reserve materials .. $1.00 per day or hour
(depending upon reserve status)

Replacement costs
for lost or damaged materials will equal
the cost of the material

To renew materials by phone call (804) 395-2433

Introduction

In recent years the subject of managing both business and personal debt and the related issue of bankruptcy has been receiving increased attention by individuals who might not previously have given the subject a passing thought. It is this writer's view that a knowledge of this subject is valuable to every thoughtful individual who, in order to survive, must cope with a world in financial turmoil. One is forced to adjust to severe economic and financial pressures comparable to the Great Depression of the 1930's with possibly worse things on the horizon.

It is not our intention to advocate declaring bankruptcy at the first sign of individual financial problems. A knowledge of bankruptcy matters and related laws may enable an individual to avoid it altogether. On the other hand we do not consider bankruptcy to be necessarily a sign of immorality, irresponsibility, or ignorance.

A review of bankruptcy reveals many famous individuals who have been outstanding in their fields. Mickey Rooney, Dick Haymes, Lance Alworth, George Sanders, Craig Morton, Pat Boone — all have experienced bankruptcy. The above individuals achieved success in careers other than business. But how do we explain that some of the most successful businessmen of all times — such as Henry Ford, Bernard Gimbel, Milton Hershey, and Frank Woolworth — had at least one experience with bankruptcy. To build the giant business enterprises, such as these individuals did, requires great courage and willingness to take risks. But individuals with these entrepreneurial characteristics do have a greater chance of going bankrupt at some time in their careers. Nor is great financial genius any guarantee against bankruptcy. One of the few investment men who foresaw the 1929 stock market crash was Bernard Baruch, a financial advisor to a number of Presidents and a man who experienced bankruptcy not once, but a number of times.

Wealthy family background is not any guarantee against bankruptcy. In one of the most spectacular bankruptcy cases in recent years a wealthy family name proved to be a key factor in causing financial disaster. In 1970 Lammot du Pont Copeland, the son of the then Chairman of the Board of the huge DuPont Company, entered bankruptcy court in a case which was to result in claims of over $50 million. A major part of Mr. Copeland's problem was that his du Pont name made it so easy for him to borrow. In most cases the debt was incurred by companies in which Mr. Copeland had an interest and signed his name to guarantee repayment.

Perhaps before you read further you'd like some insight on what lies ahead.

The first part of the book deals with some of the relevant economic background that we consider necessary to put the problem of bankruptcy in perspective. Part of the material is historical, but much of it deals with broad economic forces that have recently aggravated financial problems of individuals and businesses. It is our view that the individual must know the size of the economic problems facing the country today if he is to avoid being caught in the accompanying financial difficulties.

After dealing with the external factors that are principal causes in economic and financial problems, then we go on to discuss the problems which individuals create for themselves. A large emphasis is placed on wise consumer purchasing decisions and personal financial management.

An entire section follows that is devoted to the subject of involuntary bankruptcy and the desirability of its avoidance. Basically the pitfalls which can trigger involuntary bankruptcy are explored in detail.

A full chapter, the fourth, reviews the subject of Wage Earners Plans, which is a method of working out of financial problems without going through bankruptcy. The procedure is described, and forms are included with explanations. Included are the most commonly asked questions and answers about this procedure.

The next major issue is voluntary bankruptcy, including basic advantages to both debtors and creditors. There is described the basic procedures to be followed and the most commonly asked questions. This book stresses various pitfalls to be avoided.

A full section, chapter six, is a detailed description of forms to be used, definitions, and procedures to be followed.

An entire chapter deals with considerations specifically involving businesses. Proprietorships, partnerships, and corporations are covered.

Throughout this book our goal is to maintain a neutral position on the subject of bankruptcy for any individual situation.

It is my view and that of my research staff, that this book will give you the necessary background information to enable you to make your own decisions, based on your particular circumstances, on HOW TO GET OUT — IF YOU'RE IN OVER YOUR HEAD!

Historical Background

The history of bankruptcy is as old as civilization itself. Reference to creditor/debtor relationships can be found in the Old Testament and scholars in the field of ancient history have found even earlier references than Moses in the Old Testament.

Much of the history of bankruptcy has been a sad commentary on humanity. In Mesopotamia, one of the earliest civilizations, a bankrupt might find himself enslaved for debt or more commonly might sell his wife or children into slavery so as to acquire the capital to pay off his debts. In Ancient Greece debt was classified as a crime comparable to murder and even in later periods debtors might be required to sell their children as slaves. Hindu law permitted a creditor to kill or maim a debtor, but he could force the debtor to work for him instead. In Ancient Rome bankruptcy was punishable by slavery or death. When the creditors disagreed on the alternative, the bankrupt could be dismembered with each creditor claiming his portion.

During the Middle Ages, punishment by death still continued. In parts of Spain as late as 1360, the money changer who was unable to pay his creditors was beheaded in front of his bank. In France punishment was particularly severe for fraudulent bankruptcy. The Code of Commerce of 1673 provided the death penalty for the fraudulent bankrupt, but the penalty was apparently not carried out immediately. A record of one such bankrupt included his being led through the street, clad only in a shirt, with a rope around his neck. He was attached to the public pillory for three days, fined heavily, and then sent to the galleys for nine years.

A history of bankruptcy would also reveal that governments, while making laws punishing debtors, were often at the root of the problem. One of the largest bankruptcies of Medieval Times was the collapse of the Fugger financial empire in 1607, after two centuries of growth. Contributing to the fall of the firm were defaults on debt by Spain and France in 1557 followed by similar defaults by the Dutch and Belgian governments in subsequent decades. Although the Fuggers did not have many outside partners, their failure ruined so many clients that a larger debtor's prison had to be built in Augsburg to hold them.

Still the history of bankruptcy has not been completely a negative story. Even when a person could be enslaved for debt, it was not necessarily for life. One of the oldest legal codes, that of Hammurabi, provided "three years shall they work in the house of the buyer and in the fourth year he shall fix their liberty." Slavery of one Hebrew by another Hebrew might also be light and temporary, as indicated by the following quote from the Old Testament. "If thy brother be waxen poor and be sold unto thee and shall serve thee six years after which he and his family were free to depart."

The Hebrew laws also provided certain protection to the debtor by ensuring that he could not be deprived of basic necessities, which offers the precedent for what we now call "exempt assets" discussed later in the book. When the Hebrew slave was set free, he was not to be "sent away empty" but furnished "liberally out of the flock, and out of the winepress," and of that which the owner had. If a person's cloak was taken from him as security as a loan, it had to be returned to him at nightfall. A creditor could not take a debtor's millstone, because this would deprive the family of its daily food.

In the early history of the United States, debtor prisons existed but the shortage of labor reduced their importance relative to Europe. The colony of Georgia was established in 1732 as a debtor's refuge. The "indentured servant" was common in our early history and represented mostly voluntary debt slaves working off their debt obligation. Starting with Kentucky in 1821, debtor prisons were abolished one by one. The Constitution gave Congress the power to establish laws on the subject of bankruptcy, and three times (1800, 1841, and 1867) Congress did enact a law, but in each case repealed it after the economic crises, that triggered the laws, passed. During most of these years state laws predominated, but these were not uniform. The present Federal Bankruptcy law was passed in 1898 and was importantly modified in 1938.

The nature of our present bankruptcy law was summarized well by a Supreme Court Justice in 1873 who said:

> The very essence of a national bankruptcy system is the doing away with pre-existing contracts, the prevention of preference among creditors, ... the distribution of assets of a debtor upon the principle that equality is equity among creditors and the making of such reasonable exemptions of property to the bankrupt as will keep him from absolute poverty, give him support and educate his family, and make him a good and useful citizen.

Although major changes in bankruptcy laws are not frequent, gradual changes do take place from time to time. Within the last several years, debtors have been given increased protection by the Consumer Credit Protection Act and Trust in Lending Act. One objective of this legislation was restricting the practice of wage garnishment, which often leads to bankruptcy.

The renewed interest in bankruptcy must come as a surprise to many government and academic economists who not too many years ago believed that economic cycles and their resultant financial crises could be controlled if not banished by the government. With the safety of bank deposits insured by the government, they have told us, there would be no danger of "runs on the banks" such as occurred during the Great Depression. Also the banks have not one, but at least three government regulatory agencies keeping check on them, so that one might reasonably be justified in thinking that our banking system is safe beyond question. Yet we shall see in chapter 7, that our banking system is in serious trouble.

The Social Security System was expected to be a guarantee that our senior citizens would not be destitute in their later years. A deduction for Social Security was supposed to be like an insurance premium. Unfortunately it has proved to be one of the most rapidly increasing taxes in recent years with no end in sight if the system is to avoid bankruptcy itself. Rapidly increasing taxes, including social security taxes, have been a major deterrent to individuals attempting to provide their own retirement funds.

Unemployment was also expected to be controllable at low levels. First government expenditures were supposed to stabilize the economy, so that wide economic swings could not occur. Secondly, an increasing percentage of our work force is employed in public and quasi-public industries, which were supposed to maintain, or even increase, employment during economic downturns. There would still be a few who were unemployed but didn't we have unemployment compensation to take care of the temporarily unemployed and welfare to take care of those unable to work for other reasons? Unfortunately these economic stabilizers have not only been overrated, they have been completely misrepresented to the citizenry of the U.S. The government has always found it politically popular to stimulate the economy by new programs but unpopular to provide for such programs on a pay-as-you-go basis, so that a deficit budget has been the rule year in and year out. Government spending has thus been destabilizing rather than stabilizing, as the latter would require the government to operate its budget at a surplus during the strong part of the economic cycle. Another myth that has recently been shattered is that government can add employees without regard to the economy and their financial situation. States and municipalities with unbalanced budgets can still hire more employees as long as their credit ratings are good enough to borrow enough to make up for the deficit which is created, but eventually lenders will not invest in the bonds of irresponsibly managed public entities. The federal government, with its power to print money to pay its bills, can postpone the day of reckoning longer than states and municipalities, but must eventually become more financially responsible if we are to avoid economic collapse and possibly revolution.

Meanwhile we can expect economic and financial problems to continue, affecting us all. In 1974 there were almost 190,000 bankruptcies and estimates for 1975 run as high as 300,000. For comparison purposes, the number was 178,000 in 1970, up from 98,000 in 1960 which in turn was an increase from only 25,000 in 1950. Nor are individuals the only cases. Reliable figures are not available on how many small businesses go broke, since many sell out, merge, or just cease operations instead of going through bankruptcy.

Large companies have not been immune to the problems of bankruptcy, either, as indicated by the financial collapse of the Penn Central Railroad and more recently W. T. Grant. Other large companies have been rumored to be near bankrupt but were rescued by special government action or behind the scenes action by our banking authorities. Perhaps most disturbing has been the financial disasters that have overcome entire industries, such as the Real Estate Investment Trusts. While the latter is not a well known industry to the average individual, its collapse has had extremely negative effects on our building industry and even the banking system itself. Governments have not been immune, with New York City appearing as perennial candidate for Bankrupt of the Year. Italy, among the Developed Nations, is a leader in the race toward bankruptcy, with Great Britain its major competition. The underdeveloped countries have many entrants to the race, with many now surviving only through the grace of the creditor nations.

The average individual may feel it hard to sympathize with the problems of major corporations or cities such as New York City. Unfortunately this is somewhat like the short sighted view of the sailor lying in his bunk who was told by an excited companion that the ship was sinking. His reply was "so what, it's not my ship." As individuals we are caught up in the problems besetting our government, our cities, and our corporations whether we like it or not. When industry has financial problems, it cannot expand capacity. On the one hand this reduces employment opportunities while on the other it leads to shortages of various products, adding to inflationary pressures. Financial problems at the government level bring about lost job opportunities, higher taxes, and a lower standard of living.

These trends are already well underway. First we have experienced escalating inflation, reducing our real standard of living as indicated in the following table and chart.

Year	Average Weekly Earnings	Cost of Living Index	Weekly Earnings Adjusted for Decline in Dollar	Spendable Average Weekly Earnings for Worker with 3 Dependents	
				In Current Dollars	In 1967 Dollars
1975	158.95 *	158.6	100.22	137.84	86.91
1974	154.45	147.7	104.57	134.37	90.97
1973	145.43	133.1	109.26	127.41	95.73
1972	136.16	125.3	108.67	121.09	96.64
1971	127.28	121.3	104.93	112.41	92.67
1970	119.46	116.3	102.72	104.61	89.95
1969	114.61	109.8	104.38	99.99	91.07
1968	107.73	104.2	103.39	95.28	91.44
1967	101.84	100.0	101.84	90.86	90.86

* As of April 1975

This decline in real spendable earnings is graphically displayed in the chart on the preceding page.

The unaware individual who earns more today than he did a few years ago may not be conscious at first of the fact that his real income has been reduced. He has also been encouraged by prevailing easy credit policies to maintain his standard of living by going deeper into debt. But this is temporary relief. The cost of carrying this debt takes an increasing share of personal income, especially since not only does the debt rise but the interest rate on each dollar of debt tends to rise during inflation just as other prices do. The following charts illustrate the rise in consumer and household debt as a percentage of disposable personal income.

CONSUMER AND HOUSEHOLD DEBT AS A PERCENTAGE OF DISPOSABLE PERSONAL INCOME

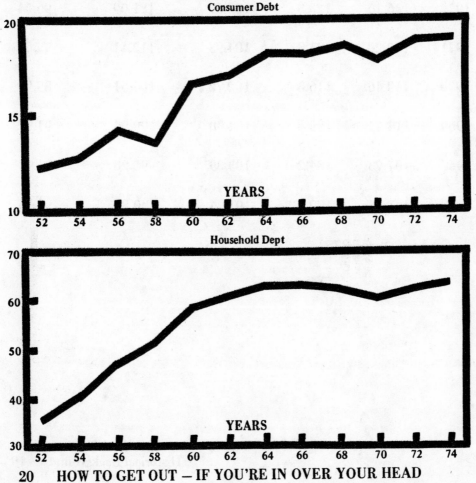

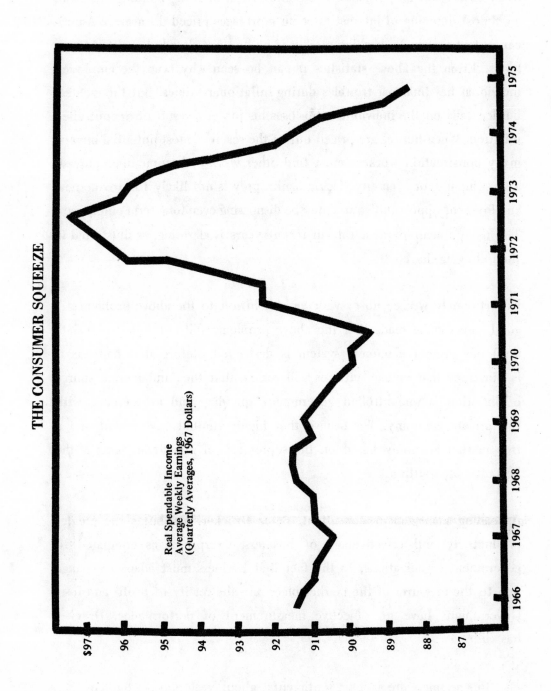

THE CONSUMER SQUEEZE

Real Spendable Income
Average Weekly Earnings
(Quarterly Averages, 1967 Dollars)

During this period the level of interest rates almost doubled, raising the cost of borrowing for all purposes. The combination of rising building costs and an almost doubling of interest rates on mortgages priced the average American out of the single dwelling market if he had not already bought at lower levels. From the above statistics it can be seen why even the employed individual has financial troubles during inflationary times. But the greatest burden falls on the individual who loses his job as a result of uncontrolled inflation. When houses are priced out of the reach of most potential buyers, many construction workers must find other work or become unemployed. The company, or even city, facing bankruptcy is not likely to provide new employment opportunities and may be dismissing even long term employees. The rising unemployment rate in recent years is alarming, as illustrated in the following charts.

Unfortunately we see no easy or early solution to the above problems. A good case can be made that the above problems will continue to escalate until our present economic system is destroyed. Before that happens it is our hope that enough citizens will realize that the fundamental source of inflation is uncontrolled government spending and interference with the private economy. We believe that highly limited government and a free market economy based on the supremacy of individual rights is the best ultimate solution.

A leading management consultant, Peter Drucker, attributes the greater productivity and effectiveness of business enterprises, as compared to government organizations, to the fact that business must adapt to change due to the pressures of the market place and the reality of profit and loss. Governments have no objective measurement of performance. Drucker has said:

Businessmen are just as sentimental about yesterday as bureau-

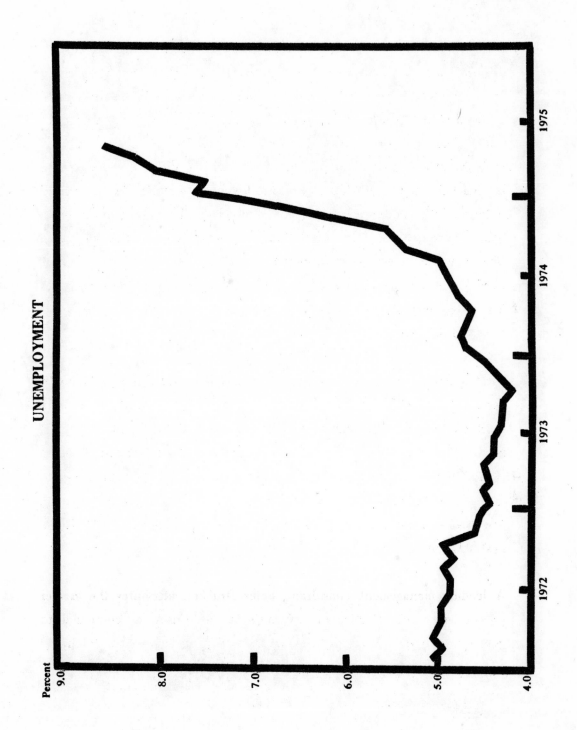

crats. They are just as reluctant to abandon anything. They are just as likely to respond to the failure of a product or program by doubling the efforts invested in it. But they are, fortunately, unable to indulge freely in their predilections. They stand under an objective discipline of the market. They have an objective outside measurement, profitability.[1]

The individual who has been alerted to these basic economic problems has better chances of survival than one who is unaware. The matter is particularly difficult as we have a combination of inflation and depression occurring simultaneously. We can be sure of recurring periods of expansion and contraction, so that we must maintain enough financial flexibility to survive the contraction periods. It is instructive to note that periods of financial irresponsibility and runaway inflation have typically been terminated by financial collapse and waves of bankruptcy. In effect the bankruptcies serve the purpose of giving the individuals, companies, and economy a fresh start. Capital is also released for use in more productive ways.

In our introduction, we referred to the question of whether or not bankruptcy is a sign of dishonesty, stupidity, or irresponsibility. While this will be discussed at other points throughout the book, the material in this chapter supports the view that any individual can be a victim of economic circumstances beyond his control. One study of bankrupts showed that at least half were beyond the individual's control, being due to reduced income, unexpected medical expenses, marital troubles, or personal liability suits.

One quarter of the bankruptcies involved lack of prudent financial management, and only 13% involved deliberate irresponsibility toward debt repayment. The bankruptcy laws do not protect a debtor when fraud is involved, as we shall see later. Instead our bankruptcy laws are based on the concept that every *honest* man deserves a fresh start.

[1]Drucker, Peter, The Age of Discontinuity, Harper & Row, 1969.

How Individuals Help Create Their Financial Problems

In chapter 1 a dismal picture is presented of the economic and financial world in which we live. But many individuals will survive and even prosper in spite of the tough times. The president of a successful company in a regulated industry known for many failures occurring in it, was asked the secret of his success. He first pointed out that his company was efficiently operated with 15% profit margins as compared to 5% for its competitors. During good times, the president explained, the company grew because times were good and so did its competitors. During bad times the company was still profitable while many competitors were unprofitable and screaming to the regulators for rate relief. During these times the successful company was able to buy up properties of its competitors at bargain rates, and was able to continue growing in that way.

What has that to do with individuals? In many ways each of us is a money making business, whether self employed or not. We have income and expenses, assets and liabilities. It is a well known fact that most small businesses go broke within a few years after being started, and a major contributing factor has been that they didn't understand financial management. An individual who has a strong financial position is always in a position to take advantage of bargains that inevitably develop during any boom and bust cycle. When he does buy on credit, he typically can get lower interest rates than the financially burdened individual. At times it may be much cheaper to buy a home than to rent, and the financially strong individual can take advantage of the situation. The examples are endless.

The two financial statements that each successful businessman must master are the income statement and the balance sheet. The income statement records the income and expenses of the business. The balance sheet is the statement of assets and liabilities of the business. The two statements are closely related as the balance sheet will tend to improve when the income statement is favorable, and deteriorate when the income statement is unfavorable. A strong balance sheet also helps the income statement as assets help create income and liabilities create expenses.

Each individual also has an income statement and balance sheet although he may not recognize them as such. The income statement is the family budget. It starts with the individual's gross income, from which various expenses must be deducted. If income exceeds expenses, the residue is savings which goes to build up his financial position. When expenses exceed income, the difference can temporarily be made up by borrowing or buying on credit. But we must stress the temporary nature of this adjustment. The following page illustrates an effective budget format.

Several features of this budget deserve special attention. Note that income is separated into regular and temporary. A common mistake of many young couples is to base their budget on two salaries even when one is known to be temporary. If the temporary income is not used for savings or reducing

BUDGET

Income

Salaries, excluding irregular overtime	$ 9,100
Interest or other regular income	100
Add temporary income	1,800
Gross Income	$11,000

Expenses

Reserve for emergencies	800
Food	2,700
Rent	2,400
Utilities	700
Furniture	400
Clothing	600
Medical	700
Insurance	600
Education	400
Transportation	600
Total Expenses	$ 9,900
Available for Savings or Debt Repayment	**$ 1,100**

debt, it can still be used for cash purchases of items not part of the regular weekly budget.

A second feature of the budget is that debt repayment is segregated from current cash expenses. Many of the expense items such as furniture are discretionary at the time of purchase. Once the purchase is made on credit, however, the payments are no longer discretionary. It is a good rule to pay cash for such items or finance them over a short period of time. In contrast a long term mortgage on a purchased house may be completely justified as it takes the place of rent which would have to be paid otherwise. Similarly payments on a car substitute for taxi and bus fare. Typically debt repayments should not be over 15% of the budget, excluding mortgage payments.

One final item deserves special attention. Many budgets survive until the unexpected happens. No provision has been made for dental emergencies, car repair, etc. Obviously these problems will occur, so some preparation is necessary. That is why a reserve for emergencies heads the list of expenses in the budget.

It is difficult to say that expenses in any one area are too high, as the circumstances of each household vary widely. It is possible, however, to make comparisons with how typical American families spend their money, based on figures from the Department of Labor surveys. In August 1974 median household income figures used in the study were $14,333, up from $12,626 a year previously. In the table on the following page this median income household is compared with two other levels, one with higher income of $20,777 and one with lower income of $9,198. The statistics are for an urban family of 4, with the male wage earner being 38 years of age.

As would be expected, the amount of money spent on the basic necessities rises at a slower rate than the increase in income. As the age of the head

	Low	Median	High
Total Income	$9,198	$14,333	$20,777
Total Family Consumption	7,318	10,880	14,976
Food	2,763	3,548	4,453
Housing	1,758	3,236	4,900
Transportation	643	1,171	1,521
Clothing	759	1,085	1,589
Personal Care	231	310	439
Medical Care	738	742	774
Other Family Consumption	423	786	1,297
Other Items	415	662	1,113
Taxes and Deductions	1,463	2,790	4,686
Social Security	553	780	787
Personal Income Tax	910	2,010	3,899

of the family increases, the amount spent on medical expenses rises while the amount spent on other items tends to be less. Families with more children tend to spend more on food and clothing. City dwellers have higher housing costs.

These relationships can be seen better when expenditures are given as a percentage of total income.

	Expenditures as Percent of Income		
	Low	Median	High
Total Family Consumption	79.6	75.9	72.1
Food	30.1	24.8	21.4
Housing	19.1	22.6	23.6
Transportation	7.0	8.2	7.3
Clothing	8.3	7.6	7.6
Personal Care	2.5	2.2	2.1
Medical Care	8.0	5.2	3.7
Other Family Consumption	4.6	5.5	6.2
Other Items	4.5	4.6	5.4
Taxes and Deductions	15.9	19.5	22.6
Social Security	6.0	5.4	3.8
Personal Income Tax	9.9	14.0	18.8

The individual who has made up his own budget can analyze what expense items, if any, are out of line with the above percentages, which can be used as broad guidelines.

A second problem may be that debt purchases have been bunched too close together, increasing debt repayment above the danger point. Restructuring of one's debt is a major element of improving an individual's financial health, and the subject will be discussed at length in later chapters.

Let us now turn to the second financial statement mentioned earlier — the balance sheet. The following illustration is an example.

Assets (Current)

Checking Account	$ 200
Savings Account	800
Insurance Cash Value	700
Total Current Assets	$ 1,700

Fixed Assets

House (appraised value)	$45,000
Car	2,000
Furniture	4,000
Total Fixed Assets	$51,000
Total Assets	$52,700

Liabilities

Installment Debt	$ 2,500
Mortgage	30,000
Total Liabilities	$32,500
Net Worth (Assets Less Liabilities)	$20,200

The person has a net worth of $20,200, most of which is a result of the value of his house exceeding the mortgage against it by $15,000 ($45,000 minus $30,000). The latter is probably due more to inflation than to savings. In spite of this substantial net worth, the above person may have trouble meeting his expenses out of current income. The balance sheet represents a sort of reserve which can be drawn on to a certain extent to meet the difference. If expenses exceeded income by $100 a month, the $1700 in current assets could be used to bridge the gap for 17 months. The equity in the home and furniture is much more difficult to utilize, so we have segregated this into fixed assets. The two basic problems with utilizing net worth to meet a shortage of income are these:

1. Net worth is a fixed finite amount so this adjustment can only be temporary.

2. Net worth produces income in one form or another, so that use of net worth aggravates the problem of income shortage. For example, the savings account may produce income of $48 per year. The equity of $15,000 in the house may produce a savings in mortgage interest payments of $100 per month.

Many financially successful individuals compute their net worth each year to see if their situation is improving or declining. The person who fails to improve the income statement and balance sheet over time is in financial danger and must be especially careful.

Avoiding Involuntary Bankruptcy

The person who is financially overextended may still be able to survive, particularly if he is a young person with a successful career underway. His future income may be expected to rise faster than expenses, if he consciously avoids the temptation to step up his cost of living each time he gets a raise. His long term future may be quite good — provided he survives the short term. This chapter is devoted to the pitfalls that the individual may encounter that could lead to involuntary bankruptcy in the short term.

We have mentioned that there are many contributing factors to bankruptcy, including divorce, sudden medical bills, lawsuits, and prolonged unemployment. However, an important contributing factor in many is the unwise use or mismanagement of one's credit. The problem of managing one's debt load is critical in one's ability to survive financial problems successfully, and this is the major subject matter of this chapter. First, we review the basic arguments for and against liberal use of credit, attempting to provide the background necessary for the individual reader to decide the level of debt with which he is comfortable or safe. Secondly, we suggest how an individual can be much more selective in his use of credit, stressing the pitfalls that are written into credit agreements. Thirdly, there is discussed the problems of becoming a bad credit risk and how to avoid it. Finally, the chapter introduces the concept of how to make yourself more bankrupt proof and avoid certain actions that may be fraudulent and/or cause your creditors to plunge you into involuntary bankruptcy.

The ability to borrow money when needed is a great asset which is unfortunately often squandered. The financially unsophisticated individual will typically pay a higher price for an item if he can buy it on credit than he would if he had to pay cash, even before adding interest charges to the credit purchase. Certain businesses owe their survival to this type of customer, who tends to think in terms of low downpayment and low monthly payments rather than total price and value received. One observer at bankruptcy proceedings has commented on the fact that among the assets may be articles such as encyclopedias bought impulsively on credit, but still in their original boxes unopened. How unlikely that they would have been bought for a much smaller amount if a significant portion of the total price had to be paid in cash.

In the last few years of rampant inflation, much attention has been drawn to the avoidance of impulse buying. Housewives have been advised to make out a list of items needed before going to the grocery store, to avoid the temptation of buying non-essential items which are bought on impulse. Similarly the widespread availability of credit cards has received considerable criticism for making the unwise use of credit too easy for the consumer. The amount of credit available to each of us is limited, just as our cash assets are limited. There is nothing wrong with buying an encyclopedia for $900 worth of credit — unless it interferes with your buying something which is needed more, such as a car necessary to get to work or funds for the monthly rent or grocery bill. What is the amount of credit that an individual should be able to incur safely? This figure varies widely among individuals, depending on health, stability of employment, prospects for salary increases, etc. One rule of thumb is that debt repayment, exclusive of mortgage, becomes excessive at 20 to 25% of income.

During inflationary times there is often heard a strong argument for heavy borrowing. The argument runs somewhat as follows: The dollar becomes worth less every year, so why not borrow today, invest in assets which will increase in value, and pay back the debt in dollars of lower purchasing power in future years. Fortunes have been made by businessmen following this simple principle. Unfortunately it is a technique that can backfire as many investors have discovered in recent years. Assets such as urban real estate and common stocks, not to mention bonds, have gone down in dollar value while the debt owed has remained the same. Meanwhile the interest rate on debt has skyrocketed, as people who lend money are smart enough to demand a higher interest rate during inflationary times. The fortunes made in the past by heavy use of debt were accomplished when investment returns were high and interest rates low. That has not been the case in recent years.

As a person gets deeper in debt the cost of borrowing rises sharply. A prime customer of a bank may be able to borrow at 8%. If his debt load were heavier, he might have to pay 18% to a finance company. As his debt load becomes extreme he might have to resort to the friendly neighborhood loan shark who charges usurious rates. Or he may be forced to buy from certain merchants who do not violate the usury laws directly but do so indirectly by charging a higher price for their merchandise, impose extra fees, or require the customer to purchase high cost credit insurance. A heavy debt load is a burden during inflationary times, not an asset.

Strategic use of debt, however, can be a great advantage. In our modern stop and go type economy, interest rates will drop during the recession phase to levels below that which would be justified by the inflation rate. One investment rule of thumb is that interest rates tend to approximate 3% plus the expected rate of inflation. If inflation was expected to be 5%, then interest rates would tend toward 8% on low risk investments. During the recession period, however, actual rates may be well below the level temporarily. This is the ideal time for borrowing if it is to be done. At this time many items will also have declined in price temporarily. Down payments and terms on major purchases, such as homes, will be very favorable compared to other times in the business cycle.

The smart borrower will not only take advantage of the business cycle to do his borrowing on advantageous terms, but will shop for loans just as he shops for goods. We have referred to the fact that bank rates will normally be lower than finance companies, but interest rates will also vary among banking institutions. The rates on different types of loans will also vary, as can be seen when we compare interest rates on mortgages, now 9%, to installment credit rates of 18% to 36%.

The smart borrower then is one who would not buy any item on credit that he would not buy for cash; he buys major items when prices and/or interest rates are low due to a slow down in the economy, and he shops for best rates. The borrower who is already overextended is not in a strategic position to take advantage of the above mentioned opportunities. Unable to buy for cash or credit from the more conservative lenders, he must turn to higher risk lenders who charge higher interest rates to compensate for the higher risk they accept. These high risk lenders have often been a source of sorrow to unwary borrowers who may sign contracts they do not understand.

Credit counselors have urged that borrowers, before signing contracts:

1. Know what interest rate is being charged. Under the truth-in-lending legislation the rate must be given in the contract. Under previous practice, the interest rate in installment credit was often stated at only about half the real rate.[*]
2. Read the entire contract before signing. Are all the blank spaces filled in? Are all charges itemized? Are all promises in writing? Do you have a copy of the contract? Are any guarantees specific in detail?

The chance for being deceived or misled are great. A salesman may promise something different from what the written contract states, but the written contract is what counts.

One acquaintance told me of being asked by a furniture dealer to sign a paper saying that a piece of furniture (which he had just ordered minutes ago) had been received in good condition. In another incident his wife signed a contract for the purchase of a mattress and found out later that she had signed a contract for the purchase of both mattress and box springs, even though the latter item had not even been discussed.

The average consumer, just by reading the contract, could have avoided the above pitfalls. Numerous pitfalls lurk in the fine print, however, and their avoidance requires some elementary legal awareness. Debtors have often been caught on the following:

1. Late payment clause — how late can payment be, without incurring a late charge?
2. Acceleration of payments — this is a very dangerous clause which says that if the borrower fails to make any payment when it is

[*]A 12% interest rate might have been stated on a $1000 loan, based on annual interest of $120 per year. This method is grossly misleading since it ignores that the average money borrowed would be only about $500.

due, then the creditor has the right to accelerate the payments and declare all of them due immediately. In some cases, the payments may be accelerated because the borrower is not taking good care of the property or even if the property is taken out of state without permission of the creditor.

3. Title retention — this clause provides that the creditor owns the property until all payments including late charges have been paid.

4. Add on purchases — this situation develops when a customer buys a new item on credit from a store before other items from the same establishment are paid for. A new contract is signed for the new item on credit plus the remaining balance on the older items. Should the borrower default he loses not just the newly purchased items but also the older ones which were largely paid for.

5. Deficiency balances — many people unable to keep up payments on a purchase end up with the article being repossessed. The transaction doesn't end there, however, as many debtors might expect. If the article is then resold for less than the balance owed, the original purchaser is still responsible for the deficiency balance.

6. Holder in due course — this clause arises when the installment buyer also signs a negotiable promissory note along with the installment contract. A negotiable note can be sold to a third party, who becomes a "holder in due course". What happens when the seller fails to live up to his end of the contract? The debtor is still obligated to pay the third party, who bought the negotiable note! The recent consumer protection acts attempt to limit these abuses.

7. Waiver of Defense — a clause which states that the buyer agrees that if he has a claim against the seller, he will not use that claim

against any finance company that buys the contract. (This is a variation of 6, but more explicit.)

8. Wage assignment — the borrower assigns a certain portion of wages to making payment to the creditor. If the borrower falls behind in payments, the creditor can obligate the employer to deduct the specified amount.

As can be seen from the above, signing a sales contract should not be a casual undertaking. Anyone who has accumulated a great deal of debt is undoubtedly vulnerable to one or a number of the above clauses, which are like traps ready to be sprung once the individual establishes himself as a bad credit risk. How does one avoid being classed as a bad credit risk? Unfortunately many factors in a person's credit rating may be beyond his direct control. Business executives and accountants tend to rank as high credit risks, while people in common labor or menial occupations tend to rank as low credit risks. However, some people tend to reduce their rating far below that which it would be otherwise by making several basic errors. For example, when a payment is going to be delayed, notify the creditor ahead of time if possible. Ideally make a partial payment rather than no payment at all. A credit manager will worry less if he sees a balance being gradually reduced than he would if the balance remains unchanged. It is better not to start patronizing a competitor, as a lender will be more tolerant if the debtor is still an active customer. Finally it is better not to make late payments to a number of creditors. Small payments particularly should be made on time, rather than establish a reputation of being late on all accounts.

Once a person becomes a bad credit risk, he has entered into a danger zone of involuntary bankruptcy. If a creditor knows that a debtor is in bad financial condition, he may try to get a headstart on other creditors by trying to collect first. An involuntary bankruptcy case can be initiated by 1 to 3 creditors depending on the amount of debtor's obligations and size of claims. They must show that within 4 months of filing their petition for involuntary bankruptcy, that the debtor has committed one or more of the following acts:

1. Conveyance, transfer, concealment, or removal by the debtor or by another with his permission, any parts of his property with intent to hinder, delay, or defraud creditors.

2. Transfer by the debtor, while insolvent, of assets to one or more creditors with intent to prefer such creditors over remaining creditors.

3. Permitting attachment, a process used at the initiation of a lawsuit by which a lien can be placed on property as security for the payment of any judgment recovered.

4. General assignment of wages — an agreement to give a creditor the right to collect a portion of a debtor's wages if a default occurs without resort to judicial process.

5. General appointment of trustees for bankruptcy.

6. Admission of the debtor, in writing, that he is bankrupt.

The first four of these acts can occur without the debtor being aware of their consequences. The first class of act mentioned above will be covered in greater length in the chapter on bankruptcy where we cover what acts can be taken to legally protect assets and which acts would be considered fraudulent in nature.

The acts mentioned in 2, 3, and 4 above are protective provisions for creditors which attempt to prevent one creditor getting better treatment than other creditors. Giving in to one creditor can produce a domino effect whereby all creditors can demand payment.

Even if the debtor eventually has to declare voluntary bankruptcy, there are important advantages over involuntary bankruptcy. With extra time at his disposal, the debtor can legally take steps to retain a greater portion of his assets, as will be seen in the chapter on bankruptcy.

Wage Earner Plan

In the last chapter we pointed out that many individuals have reasonably good financial prospects, provided they can survive the short term. The major problem of debt can often be solved by lengthening payment time.

It is a sound principle in corporate finance to sell on favorable finance terms, and the auto and home building industries owe much of their past growth to the simple technique of enabling consumers to pay for their products over longer periods of time.

Finance companies take advantage of this principle by urging consumers with large monthly debt repayments to apply for a debt consolidation loan. A longer debt repayment period at a reduced single payment can permit the retirement of debt over a long period of time. Unfortunately, many debtors, encouraged by the lower monthly payment, immediately go further into debt, so that the relief is only temporary. Also the new debt consolidation loan may have a very high interest rate so that most of the monthly payment goes to pay interest rather than repay principal.

An alternative to the above situation is protection of the debtor under Chapter 13 of the bankruptcy law. This is known as the *wage earner's plan*, and is available to any person whose principal income is from wages, salaries, or commissions. Debts are not wiped out, but they can be settled in some cases at less than the full amount. Generally debts are stretched out over 36 months. The person is technically not a bankrupt case and the petition which he files refers to him as a debtor. Debts are to be paid from future income, in contrast to bankruptcy proceedings where a person's assets with certain important exceptions will be liquidated to pay debts, to the extent possible from the proceeds.

The use of the wage earner plans, instead of bankruptcy, has its opponents and its defenders. The advantage of the straight bankruptcy route is that a person gets a fresh start and is relieved of the burden of most obligations. In contrast the 36 month repayment period in the wage earner's plan is a long time during which the debtor's standard of living will be restricted by debt repayment. Interestingly wage earner plans are most commonly used in rural or small town communities where bankruptcy still has a strongly negative image, which this writer believes is unjustified. The difficulty of surviving the long period of restraint shows up in the fact that over half of the Chapter 13 cases fail because the debtor does not keep up payments. Surveys have shown that a large percentage of Chapter 13 debtors have had previous experience with either straight bankruptcy or a wage earner plan.

Nevertheless the wage earner's plan does have important advantages that cannot be denied. First it may be more effective in reforming debtors than some critics believe. One survey showed that only 38% of first time participants in a wage earner's plan successfully completed the plan whereas the percentage jumped to over 65% for individuals filing for a second time or more. From the debtor's viewpoint, he gains immediate protection from creditor harrassment. Once a petition for relief is filed, a court order may be sent to each and every creditor restricting them from garnishing wages or attaching assets. Exorbitant interest and credit charges will be disallowed. Certain disputed claims may be dismissed. It forces debtors to learn elementary budgeting and to exercise restraint in spending.

Strangely enough the debtor electing the wage earner plan could probably get more relief than he usually asks for. The debtor's plan usually provides for payments of debts at 100% on the dollar, asking only for an extension of time to pay the debts. However, the debtor can petition for a plan that pays considerably less than 100% for each dollar of debt, in which case his plan is called a "composition" of his debts. Whether creditors will agree with such a plan depends on the bargaining power of the debtor. If the debtor has no assets or mostly assets which would be retained in spite of bankruptcy, the creditors may very well prefer accepting a composition rather than getting nothing as a result of straight bankruptcy.

The first step in the proceeding is for the debtor to develop a plan for paying debts, to be submitted to the Court. The table on the following page is the type of information which is used in filing one's petition.

Note that estimated future monthly expenses of family does *not* include debts to be paid under the plan, as these are included in the last item on the budget (d), total amount to be paid each month under plan. However, payments on secured debts not covered by the plan would be listed under expenses. For example, a creditor who has a chattel mortgage on the debtor's car may not agree with the plan since he may be better off to repossess.

If monthly income exceeds monthly expenses, the difference is available

EXAMPLE OF A HOUSEHOLD BUDGET

(a) Give estimated average future monthly income for each spouse whether single or joint petition is filed unless spouses are separated and a single petition is filed.

    (1) Husband's monthly take-home pay $500

    (2) Wife's monthly take-home pay 300

    (3) Other monthly income (specify) . . . .———

    Total $800

(b) Give estimated average future monthly expenses of family (not including debts to be paid under plan), consisting of:

    (1) Rent or home mortgage payment (include lot rental for trailer) $200

    (2) Utilities (Electricity $30.00 Heat $50.00 Water $10.00 Telephone $10.00) 100

    (3) Food 250

    (4) Clothing 20

    (5) Laundry and cleaning 20

    (6) Newspapers, periodicals, and books (including school books) 10

    (7) Medical and drug expenses 10

    (8) Insurance (not deducted from wages): (a) Auto $20.00 (b) Other $10.00 30

    (9) Transportation (not including auto payments to be paid under plan) . . . . —

    (10) Recreation. 20

    (11) Club and union dues (not deducted from wages). . . . . —

    (12) Taxes (not deducted from wages) . . . . —

    (13) Alimony, maintenance, or support payments . . . . —

    (14) Other payments for support of dependents not living at home. . . . . —

    (15) Other (specify): . . . .———

    Total $660

(c) Excess of estimated future monthly income (last line of Item (a) above) $140

(d) Total amount to be paid each month under plan. . . . .$120 for debt repayment. To calculate this, all debts are added, not including those secured by chattel mortgages as mentioned above. The total debt figure is then increased by 10% to allow for estimated court costs, and this figure is divided by 36 — the typical period in months selected for debt repayment. This figure is compared with the one in item (c), excess of estimated future monthly income over estimated future expenses. If item (c), income after expenses, is larger than item (d) the amount to be paid each month, the plan can succeed. If income after expenses is not greater than the figure for debt repayment, reduce the debt repayment figure by various percentages. This could range to as much as 80 to 90% or as little as 10 to 20%, depending on how much of a reduction is necessary to permit income after expenses to cover debt repayment. It is vital to keep the *same* percentage of proposed debt reduction for *all* creditors. This plan with the reduced amount can then be proposed to creditors. If they do not accept the plan, serious consideration can then be given to voluntary bankruptcy. When you advise your creditors that you wish to pay your debts in full or as large a percentage as possible that you can handle and that your alternative is bankruptcy, the tendency can often be for them to accept the offer.

Unsecured creditors must receive equal treatment in the plan. If one is to be paid 80 cents on the dollar, then all are to be treated that way. *Secured creditors* have to be negotiated with separately, and they may be able to enforce their claims completely since they can repossess property covered by the debt. Should the value of the property be worth less than the amount of the debt, however, the debtor is in an excellent position to negotiate with even the secured creditor. The plan may also provide for payment of "priority" claims. These might include taxes, wages due an employee of the debtor, and rent owed for the most recent four months.

If the majority of creditors agree, the plan is submitted to the court for approval. If the plan appears reasonable, the debtor may not even be required to attend the meeting where the plan is examined. Most creditors, even though notified of the meeting, do not attend. A plan must be approved by a majority of the unsecured creditors and by each of the secured creditors whose claim is dealt with in the plan.

A set of forms which can be used in filing for the Wage Earner Plan can be bought at a cost of $4.95 from Enterprise Publishing Co., Suite 508, Beneficial Building, Wilmington, Delaware 19801. A set would include the following:

1. Instruction Sheet
2. Original Petition Under Chapter XIII
3. Statement of Affairs
4. Plan
5. Creditor's List
6. Worksheets
7. Heavy duty envelopes and covers

The Original Petition Under Chapter XIII statement is largely self explanatory, and a copy is attached. Comments on filling out the form are in italics

The second part of the form set is a 6 page statement of affairs which requests the following information:

1. Name and residence
2. Occupation and Income
3. Dependents
4. Budget (reproduced earlier in the chapter)
5. Payment of Attorney
6. Tax Refunds
7. Bank Accounts and Safety Deposit Boxes
8. Prior Bankruptcy

In re *(Insert your name in Capital Letters. List other names used in last 6 years –*
a woman married during period would list full maiden name after married
name – a businessman would include name of business or partnership.)

Debtor, Soc. Sec. No.
[Include here all names used by bankrupt within last 6 years.]

BANKRUPTCY NO. *(Leave blank)*

ORIGINAL PETITION
UNDER
CHAPTER XIII

1. Petitioner's post-office address is

2. Petitioner has his *principal place of employment — residence — domicile* within this district.
   (Inapplicable italicized words should be crossed out.)

3. No bankruptcy case initiated on a petition by or against petitioner is now pending.

4. Petitioner is qualified to file this petition and is entitled to the benefits of Chapter XIII of the Bankruptcy Act

5. Petitioner is *insolvent — unable to pay his debts as they mature.*

6. *A copy of petitioner's proposed plan is attached.*

7. *Petitioner intends to file a plan pursuant to Chapter XIII of the Act.*

Wherefore petitioner prays for relief under Chapter XIII of the Act.

Signed: ....
Attorney for Petitioner

Address: ....

....

....
Petitioner
[Petitioner signs if not represented by attorney]

STATE OF   County of   **ss.**

I,   the petitioner named in the foregoing petition, do
hereby swear that the statements contained therein are true according to the best of my knowledge, information, and belief.

(Sign in front of notary public)   ....
Petitioner

Subscribed and sworn to before me on

....

....
Official Character

9. Foreclosures, Executions, and Attachments
10. Repossessions and Returns
11. Debts
12. Codebtors
13. Property

At the end of the statement is a place for the petitioner to sign in the presence of a Notary Public. The Statement of Affairs is similar to that filed for Bankruptcy, and instructions for completing this form are covered in Chapter 6.

In addition to the Original Petition Under Chapter XIII and the Statement of Affairs, a form entitled Chapter 13 Plan must be completed. This plan is primarily based on the budget information included in the Statement of Affairs, and a copy of the form Chapter 13 Plan follows.

Two terms used in the form require some explanation, the term "priority claims" and the term "executory contract". For definition of priority claims, the reader should refer to the discussion in Chapter 6 regarding Schedule A-1 of the Bankruptcy Forms. The term "executory contract" refers to a contract that obligates the debtor to pay in the future for some future service. For example, if you have signed a contract to buy a T.V. set but have not received it yet, you need not list the debt *except* under the section "executory contracts". Leases may also fall under this category. If an attorney is used by the petitioner, a form Statement of Compensation must be submitted, signed by the attorney.

Some important differences between Wage Earner Plans and Bankruptcies should be stressed.
1. Bankruptcies are a quicker way to resolve financial problems, since Wage Earner Plans are stretched out over a period, typically

In re

BANKRUPTCY NO.

Debtor, Soc. Sec. No.
[Include here all names used by bankrupt within last 6 years.]

CHAPTER XIII
PLAN

1. The future earnings of the debtor are submitted to the supervision and control of the court and the *debtor — debtor's employer* shall pay to the trustee the sum of **$**   *weekly — semi-monthly — monthly.*

2. From the payments so received, the trustee shall make disbursements as follows:

(*a*) The priority payments required by Rule 13-309(a).

(*b*) After the above payments, dividends to secured creditors whose claims are duly proved and allowed as follows:

(*c*) *Subsequent to — pro rata with* dividends to secured creditors, dividends to unsecured creditors whose claims are duly proved and allowed **as follows:**

3. The following executory contracts of the debtor are rejected:

4. Title to the debtor's property shall revest in the debtor *on confirmation of a plan — upon dismissal of the case after confirmation pursuant to Rule 13-215 — upon closing of the case pursuant to Bankruptcy Rule 514.*

Dated:

....
Debtor

Acceptances may be mailed to

....

....
Post Office Address

36 months.

2. A large percentage of Wage Earner Plans fail to succeed, whereas a high percentage of bankruptcy plans are completed.

3. Wage Earner Plans are not subject to the rule that they can only be undertaken every 6 years as is the case with bankruptcy.

4. Wage Earner Plans look to a person's future earnings to pay off debts, whereas bankruptcy looks to a person's assets. The amount of assets that a person has becomes a major factor in the decision to go the Wage Earner route or to choose bankruptcy.

5. The majority of Wage Earner Plans are filed by the main wage earner in the family, although income of the spouse is included in the budgeting figures. In the case of bankruptcy, it may be advantageous for each to file for bankruptcy.

6. The Wage Earner Plan is in most cases easier to handle by the layman himself than bankruptcy, since the latter involves more legal advice to protect assets while not committing fraudulent acts. The cost of filing fees is also lower, being an initial fee of $15 with an additional fee of up to $15 to cover the cost of the Referee System.

Although the wage earner plan is a long term affair compared to bankruptcy, this is not altogether a disadvantage since a person has a chance to develop better ability at making budgetary and financial decisions. Typically the plan has considerable flexibility, as trustees realize that a person cannot completely live in a financial straitjacket. The court assumes that there must be some extra income in excess of the required financial payments and probably would not approve a plan that did not provide for this. A person can still buy items on credit, but the amount must not exceed his obvious limits. Although the time period is typically 36 months, extensions can be obtained when unforeseen circumstances arise. In summary the wage earner plan can be a successful plan for the financially pressed individual who just needs more time and less harrassment to work things out. It can be a much more effective plan if the individual is in a good position to get a reduction of his debts (a composition) rather than just an extension of time to pay his debts. As commented on earlier, most creditors would find it advantageous to accept reduced payments rather than see a person declare bankruptcy, where the unsecured creditor typically receives very little, if anything.

Questions and Answers Regarding A Wage Earner Plan

Q. Does the Court take a person's pay check?

A. Generally funds are collectible from the employee, but if agreeable to both employer and employee, the required amount may be sent directly to the Court. In some cases the entire pay check may be sent to the Court, which deducts the amount required for debt repayment and sends the remainder to the employee.

Q. What is the average size of the Wage Earner Plan case?

A. In the 1971 Brookings Study, the average case had $500 of assets and $2500 of debt, payable to 7 creditors. On the surface, it would appear advantageous to use the bankruptcy route. However, a substantial amount of the above debt was probably secured debt which would not be cancelled out without the debtor losing assets, many of which would have to be replaced.

Q. Does electing the wage earner plan eliminate the option of declaring bankruptcy if the plan doesn't work out?

A. No. A great many Wage Earner Plans are converted into bankruptcy cases, when the payment schedule cannot be kept. An additional filing fee of $50 is necessary to file bankruptcy. Even though the Wage Earner Plan is often unsuccessful, it may still have given the debtor additional time to improve his position to retain more under bankruptcy.

Q. What does the Wage Earner Plan do to a person's ability to get credit?

A. During the early part of the Plan, ability to get credit will possibly be reduced somewhat, since there is the possibility that the plan will fail and the debtor will then declare bankruptcy. However, it is probably best that credit not be so readily available, as easy credit is typically an important part of the debtor's problem. As the plan progresses and appears to be successful, the individual's credit rating would be improved.

Bankruptcy

Up to this point, we have stressed that a knowledge of bankruptcy can be a valuable aid just in avoiding the need to petition for bankruptcy.

At this point we consider the possibility that alternative solutions to financial problems appear to be unworkable or at least difficult, so that the advantages and disadvantages of declaring bankruptcy will be considered directly. In this chapter we first review the psychological and financial factors that must be considered in arriving at a decision to declare bankruptcy. We then outline the basic strategies of preparing for bankruptcy so that a maximum of assets can be retained. The basic procedure is then discussed, and then we cover the most commonly asked questions about bankruptcy. Preparation of forms is deferred until Chapter 6.

Declaring bankruptcy is not strictly a financial decision, but also an important psychological one. Before going into the strategy of making one's self bankruptcy-proof as possible, some consideration should be given to the non-financial personal aspects of the decision. One frequent observer of bankruptcy cases has commented on how surprising it is that many petitioners wait so long before doing so. One of the most complete academic studies devoted to bankruptcy[1] included questionnaires with questions regarding attitudes of Americans toward bankruptcy. Interviewees, for example, were asked what they would think of doing business with a person that had gone bankrupt. Approximately 26% indicated that they would be reluctant or cautious, and would prefer to do business elsewhere. The interviewees were also asked how they would feel about going bankrupt. Approximately 33% said they would go bankrupt only as a last resort, and another 20% indicated that they would not go bankrupt — they would rather die! Another 18% said they would feel disgraced.

While the above results indicate the distaste that Americans have for bankruptcy, it is interesting to note that most people who have gone through bankruptcy feel better for having done so. Of those interviewed, well over half said they were better off, with approximately one quarter indicating that they were much better off. When asked about their current financial position as compared to "before bankruptcy", two thirds indicated they were better off with half of this group saying that they were "much better off". One could conclude that bankruptcy is not nearly as negative an experience as most Americans believe. In general the relief from burdensome debt and creditor harassment more than offsets any feelings of failure generated by going bankrupt.

The negative feeling toward bankruptcy is stronger in rural and small towns where the relation between creditor and debtor is less impersonal than in more urban areas. The negative feeling also tends to vary, depending upon

[1]Stanley, David T. and Girth, Marjorie, Bankruptcy, Problems, Process, Reform, The Brookings Institution, 1971.

the state of the economy. During the depression of the 1930's, unemployment and underemployment were so widespread that a person's financial failures could be attributed to the economy, not his own personal shortcomings.[1] In recent years the economy is once again experiencing violent contractions in area after area, in spite of all the so-called economic stabilizers, such as social security and unemployment compensation. The fear and distrust of bankruptcy is likely to decline under present circumstances.

A review of the history of bankruptcy and a study of present bankruptcy laws would lead to the following conclusions.

1. Historically laws which favored punishment of debtors were not only inhumane, but produced little value to the creditor while doing great harm to the debtor.

2. Problems, including financial ones, come upon everyone and sometimes are overwhelming. In the battle of life anyone can get knocked down, many times, and criticism possibly could be restricted to those who don't try to get back up.

3. Many creditors deserve little sympathy if they experience some losses in bankruptcy cases. They are aware of risks and build a loss reserve into their prices. Any business that sells on credit charges interest[2] and interest rates charged on different type debts vary with the risk involved. Interest on installment credit is sufficiently high to pay for a lot of bankruptcy losses.

4. Present bankruptcy laws do not protect the dishonest debtor, due to the many restrictions against fraud contained in the law. The feeling that being a former bankrupt implies dishonesty is completely unwarranted.

---

[1]An acquaintance tells me that during the depression his family received a letter from the Finance Company asking "What would your neighbors think if we sent a truck out and repossessed all your furniture?" To which the father replied "They would think you were a bunch of S.O.B.'s." The Finance Company did, and the neighbors did.

[2]Sometimes no interest is directly charged but the price of goods sold is adjusted upward over what would be charged otherwise.

From an objective view point, there is no reason to feel inadequate or dishonest because of bankruptcy. This attitude developed in rural America in a less complex economic period and was not even justified then. It is certainly unjustified now as an individual's destiny is often controlled by factors beyond his control. These include actions of Big Government, Big Labor, and sometimes Big Business.

Turning from the psychological to the financial side, the decision to go bankrupt should be importantly influenced by the possibility that the Wage Earner Plan may be more attractive as an alternative. This might be true if debts could comfortably be paid off over a three year period. If not a person should consider declaring bankruptcy, but only after rearranging assets and liabilities so as to salvage as much as possible.

First there are some debts which are not discharged by bankruptcy, including the following:

1. Taxes of the United States, the state, county, district, and municipality in which the bankrupt resides, not more than 3 years old.
2. Liabilities for obtaining property by false pretenses or false representations, for obtaining money by a false financial statement.
3. Alimony and child support.
4. Debts which are not listed on the schedules.
5. Liabilities for malicious injuries to the person or property of another.

The bankruptcy act prescribes a certain order of payment of the several classes of creditors out of the net amount of property left after the segregation of property belonging to adverse claimants, secured creditors, and the exemptions, and after the payment of expenses of the individual sales.

The order of priority is as follows:

1. Administrative expenses.
2. Wages to wage-earners, earned within 3 months before bankruptcy proceedings and not to exceed $600 for each claimant.
3. Taxes.
4. Debts owing to any person entitled to priority.
5. Rent owing to a landlord, accrued within 3 months prior to bankruptcy.

Another class of debts would be secured claims, and these require special attention during bankruptcy proceedings. A secured debt is one for which the creditor holds property that offers security that the debt will be paid. Much consumer installment credit is in this category. The seller does not retain the property but retains the right to repossess it if the buyer defaults. If the value of the security is more than the debt, the court will turn it over to the creditor. To the extent that the debt exceeds the value of the article, this excess will be recognized by the court but only as an unsecured debt.

All other debts are unsecured and these bear the bulk of losses during bankruptcy.

Prior to going bankrupt, the debtor typically has money to pay only part of his bills. If the choice is between paying against an unsecured debt or against debts which will not be discharged, it is to the debtor's advantage to favor the latter claims. In the case of secured property where the debt is greater than the value of the security, the article will be repossessed. Often, however, the debtor can retain the item by making a new contract at a new price approximating resale value after the bankruptcy. *He should not after bankruptcy make any payment on old contracts as this could revive the debts!*

Prior to bankruptcy the debtor should concentrate on paying bills on those items which can be retained after bankruptcy. An "exempt" item or asset is property which can be retained after bankruptcy, being exempt from seizure to satisfy debts, and does not have to be surrendered to the bankruptcy courts for payment of creditors of a bankrupt. However, if the exempt item is obtained by incurring a debt, its exempt status does not prevent its being recovered by the seller. Specific exemptions are determined by state law and vary widely, but include such items as apparel, working tools, home furnishing, domestic animals, life insurance, and salary and wages up to a limit. The amount of exemptions can vary from a few thousand dollars up to fifty thousand dollars and more depending on the state of residence. One advisor in bankrupt cases has even suggested that a person with considerable assets and considering bankruptcy relocate to a state with favorable exemption treatment. Since residency is determined by where he spent the greater part of the last six months, it would only take 3 months and 1 day to satisfy residency requirements. For details on state exemptions, refer to Appendix.

The importance of exempt assets to the bankrupt individual can hardly be overemphasized. They offer the base upon which to rebuild one's financial status. Any person considering bankruptcy should put as much of his assets in these areas as possible. Partly this will consist of paying bills on exempt items where money is owed against them. In other cases a simple switch of funds from a checking account into a Federal Savings & Loan (in some states) or into an insurance policy with cash value (exempt in most states) or simply the purchase of an exempt article will be a strategic move.

The major asset of many individuals is the equity in one's home, and the best protection for this asset is homesteading it. Homesteading prevents the seizure of a home for any debts except those for which you have pledged the property, such as the mortgage. Here again state laws vary widely, from $40,000 in North Dakota to none in certain states. Generally the Western states are most liberal. In many states only a "head of the family" can qualify for homestead exemption. A married man would qualify, and usually a divorced or widowed man or woman with children under 18 living with them would also qualify. Generally the property claimed for homestead must be the principal residence of the bankrupt. Homesteading must take place before petitioning for bankruptcy, and information as to forms to be filed for homesteading can generally be obtained at the local County Clerk or County Recorder's Office. Homestead exemption laws are summarized in the Appendix. Some sample homestead forms are as follows.

Declaration by husband

I, _____, hereby declare:

I am the head of a family, I am married, and my wife's name is _____ _____. My family consists of my wife and _____ children.

At the time of making this declaration of homestead, I actually reside with my family on premises located in the County of _____, State of _____, more particularly described as follows: _____.

I claim and declare the premises, with the dwelling house _____ [and outbuildings] on it, and its appurtenances, as a homestead for the joint benefit of myself and my wife and family.

_____ [No former declaration of homestead had been made by me or by my wife, either jointly or separately *or* A former declaration of homestead has been made by _____, but it was abandoned before the execution of this declaration of homestead.]

I estimate the actual cash value of the premises to be _____ Dollars ($____).

Executed on _____, 19___

[Signature]

[Acknowledgment]

Declaration by wife

I, _____, hereby declare:

I am a married woman, and my husband's name is _____. My husband is the head of a family, consisting of my husband and myself _____ [and _____ children].

At the time of making this declaration of homestead, I actually reside on the premises described below with my husband _____ [and family], and I claim and declare the premises, with the dwelling house _____ [and outbuildings], and the appurtenances on it, as a homestead for the joint benefit of myself and my husband _____ [and family].

The premises on which I reside with my husband _____ [and family] are located in the County of _____, State of _____, and are described as follows: _____ *[legal description]*.

_____ [No former declaration of homestead has been made by me or by my husband, jointly or separately *or* A former declaration of homestead has been made by _____, but it was abandoned before the execution of this declaration of homestead.] I estimate the actual cash value of the premises to be _____ Dollars ($____).

Executed on _____, 19___.

                                            [Signature]

[Acknowledgment]

Joint declaration by husband and wife

We, _____ and _____, hereby declare:

We are husband and wife. I, _____ [name of husband], am the head of a family, consisting of myself and my wife _____ [and _____ children].

At the time of making this declaration, we actually reside _____ [with our family] on the premises described below, and we claim and declare the premises, with the dwelling house _____ [and outbuildings] on it, and its appurtenances, as a homestead for our joint benefit _____ [and for the benefit of our family].

The premises on which we so reside _____ [with our family] are located in the County of _____, State of _____, and are described as follows: _____ *[legal description]*.

_____ [No former declaration of homestead has been made by either of us, jointly or severally *or* A former declaration of homestead has been made by _____ _____, but it was abandoned before the execution of this declaration of homestead.]

We estimate the actual cash value of the premises to be _____ Dollars ($____).

Executed on _____, 19___.

                                            [Signatures]

[Acknowledgment]

While rearranging one's assets in preparation for bankruptcy, one must be extremely careful not to commit fraudulent acts. An honest error or omission without intent to defraud can be corrected. To lie or seek to cheat in a bankruptcy proceeding is a crime, and not only would be grounds for denial of the petition for discharge of debts but also could result in a fine and/or imprisonment for those committing fraud.

The destruction, falsification, or concealment of records about the bankrupt's financial condition by the bankrupt can also be grounds for denial. Not every petitioner for bankruptcy is expected to have books, particularly individuals not in business for themselves. In most cases, salaried employees and wage earners do not have to keep books and records in order to receive a discharge. If a bankrupt has kept books, however, they should be produced.

A person may also be denied a discharge if he has obtained credit by a material false statement in writing that misrepresents his financial position. This is a particularly treacherous pitfall. When applying for credit, an individual may fill out a form which has a space for listing present debts. Typically he may list his major debts but due to lack of space or slip of memory, omit minor debts — particularly those he considers trivial. The creditor may claim that he gave credit to the debtor based on the claim that this was a false statement. Even if the debtor receives general approval of his bankruptcy petition, the creditor may still sue, arguing that this debt was not dischargeable because of misrepresentation. One credit counselor advises people, when filling out credit forms, to include a figure for miscellaneous small debts, not listed specifically. If a person has already bought an item based upon a credit form in which he omitted certain debts, he would be better off to pay for this item before declaring bankruptcy, as any evidence of fraud might undermine his entire case.

Another temptation that the debtor should avoid, when contemplating bankruptcy, is the attempt to salvage property by concealing or transferring property to others, such as friends or relatives, without receiving adequate consideration (payment). To be grounds for denial of discharge the action must occur within 12 months immediately preceding the filing of the petition and must be done with intent to hinder or defraud creditors. The transfer, to be fraudulent, would also have to be done when the person was already insolvent or made insolvent by the gift. To avoid this pitfall, a person must receive fair payment for any item transferred to another. The payment does not have to be money, but can be another article or even cancellation of a debt which the debtor owes to the other individual, but such a debt would have to be definite and provable. Failure to list a significant asset would probably be tolerated by the court, if it was an honest oversight and not intended to defraud, but a deliberate failure to list assets would be reason to bar a discharge. The creditor only has to show that the assets existed and are not accounted for. The debtor then has the burden of proving that the assets were not concealed, destroyed, or transferred with the intent to defraud. A person's gifts during the previous 12 months to a spouse would be carefully checked. If the person were not insolvent at the time of gift, there would be no grounds for considering the transfer fraudulent. However, a gift should not be made within 4 months of filing a petition for bankruptcy, under any circumstances.

Other grounds for denying a bankruptcy petition include a restriction on filing bankruptcy in less than 6 years after a previous bankruptcy and deliberate failure to obey court orders, and non-payment of filing fees.

Up to this time, we have only discussed preparing for bankruptcy. If the person feels he is safe from the pitfalls discussed above, he is now ready for the actual event. Probably the first question to be faced is whether a lawyer should be retained. Here a wide difference of opinion exists. One writer on the subject of bankruptcy, a non-lawyer, comments that he would approach a court of law without a lawyer with the same enthusiasm that he would have for removing his own appendix. In contrast another writer, a lawyer himself, takes a more balanced view. His advice would be to have a lawyer if a person has substantial assets to protect, particularly a home. However, he concludes that a person could do it himself if he had no assets and were not in business. In one extensive study of bankruptcy, the researchers concluded that clients without lawyers were at a disadvantage in negotiating with creditors.

Nevertheless the study was very critical of the counselors for very poor performance, although only 10% of the debtors were critical of their attorneys. In many cases the amount of legal work is limited to filling out the forms and making one appearance in court, for which services the bankrupt can be expected to pay a minimum of about $300.00. The preparation of forms is covered in Chapter 6 for those interested in filing their own petitions. The information for the forms is supplied by the debtor. In many courts the clerks, while they cannot give legal advice, know much more about filling out forms than most lawyers and are willing to help. As for the appearance in court, most personal bankruptcy cases are fairly routine. A judge (called a referee) asks questions about items contained in the petitions, and may ask questions about dispositions of property. He is not an opponent of the bankrupt, but is only asking questions to get the information he needs. On routine cases, the first meeting can be over in far less than an hour. For do-it-yourselfers, the first step is to obtain a set of legal forms such as described in Chapter 6. A filing fee of $50 is required. After receiving the petition for bankruptcy, the court clerk mails out to all creditors a notice of the hearing known as the first meeting of creditors. Typically the time for the meeting is 10 to 30 days from the date on which the petition was filed. When a bankrupt's name is called, he takes the witness stand. If the case is complex, the judge (referee) may appoint a trustee to conserve the assets, check for other assets, and make equitable distribution to the creditors. The latter have a certain time to object to the debtor receiving a discharge of his debts. If a creditor does object in writing, a hearing is held to determine the validity of the claim. After discharge, creditors are restrained from any further attempts to collect debts, and a violation of this restraint is contempt of court.

Commonly Asked Questions About Bankruptcy

Q. Need I be employed?

A. No, since any debt repayment is to come from liquidation of assets, not from income. Actually unemployment is a major cause of bankruptcy.

Q. Are my rights as a citizen affected?

A. No. A person can still vote, get licenses, own property, engage in business, receive unemployment compensation if out of work, etc.

Q. What if I don't have the necessary cash to pay the fee?

A. The fee can be paid in installments, by filing an additional form requesting this.

Q. Where can I get help if I don't have funds for a lawyer?

A. A lawyer may be agreeable to receiving his fee in installments, so a large amount of cash may not be necessary. It may be possible to hire a lawyer on an hourly basis, so that the expense will be reduced if you do much of the clerical work yourself and use his time for answering legal questions, checking the forms, and appearing with you in court. If you are below federal poverty guidelines, you may be able to obtain assistance from the Legal Aid Society.

Q. When is bankruptcy effective?

A. As soon as the individual files for bankruptcy, he is temporarily relieved from payment of debts, so that in this sense it is effective immediately. The situation becomes permanent when the court issues a discharge.

Q. What do I do if a creditor keeps calling after I petition for bankruptcy?

A. A creditor cannot prevent you from filing for bankruptcy. After the forms are filed, the court should notify your creditors. If one does call, tell him you are bankrupt and give him the case number. If you are harassed, you may be able to sue successfully. After bankruptcy, do not make any payment on a debt that has been discharged, as this could revive the debt. To avoid this possibility, one advisor suggests that no business be done with a former creditor.

Q. What responsibilities does a person have for his relatives' debts?

A. For the most part, none. In the case of minor children, there would be little reason to go bankrupt since they are for the most part not legally liable for debts. In the case of a wife, the situation is more complex. If she signed for your debts, as is common in purchase of major items, she shares responsibility. Your responsibility for debts which she may have run up on her own depends on whether necessities or luxuries were bought. There is generally no responsibility for other relatives.

Filling Out The Forms

Most people have had some exposure to filling out government forms and might justifiably assume that filling out a set of bankruptcy forms would be a complex task. While legal terms cannot be avoided in such documents, the forms are relatively straight forward and include clear cut instructions for completion. The forms have been in existence for years with relatively little change, as bankruptcy law has undergone little change in recent decades. An individual looking at bankruptcy forms now in existence would find little change in format or instructions from forms in existence 20 or more years ago. Most changes which have occurred have simplified the procedure.

Altogether there are a total of 30 official bankruptcy forms that are used in different situations. They are listed on the following page.

Fortunately not all forms would have to be submitted in any given bankruptcy. Innovative publishers of legal forms have also reduced the number

OFFICIAL BANKRUPTCY FORMS

[Note — These official forms should be observed and used with such alterations as may be appropriate to suit the circumstances.]

Form
No. 1.   Petition for Voluntary Bankruptcy
No. 2.   Application To Pay Filing Fees in Installments
No. 3.   Order Permitting Payment of Filing Fees in Installments
No. 4.   Verification on Behalf of a Corporation
No. 5.   Verification on Behalf of a Partnership
No. 6.   Schedules
No. 7.   Statement of Affairs for Bankrupt Not Engaged in Business
No. 8.   Statement of Affairs for Bankrupt Engaged in Business
No. 9.   Creditors' Petition for Bankruptcy
No. 10. Summons to Bankrupt
No. 11. Adjudication of Bankruptcy
No. 12. Order for First Meeting of Creditors and Related Orders, Combined with Notice Thereof and of Automatic Stay
No. 13. General Power of Attorney
No. 14. Special Power of Attorney
No. 15. Proof of Claim
No. 16. Proof of Claim for Wages, Salary, or Commissions
No. 16A. Proof of Multiple Claims for Wages, Salary, or Commissions
No. 17. Order Approving Election of Trustee or Appointing Trustee and Fixing the Amount of his Bond
No. 18. Notice to Trustee of his Election or Appointment and of Time for Filing a Complaint Objecting to Discharge of Bankrupt
No. 19. Bond of Trustee or Receiver
No. 20. Order Approving Trustee's Bond
No. 21. Order That No Trustee Be Appointed
No. 22. Report of Exempt Property
No. 23. Order Approving Report of Exemptions
No. 24. Discharge of Bankrupt
No. 25. Caption for Adversary Proceeding
No. 26. Summons and Notice of Trial of Adversary Proceeding
No. 27. Subpoena to Witness
No. 28. Notice of Appeal to a District Court from a Judgment or Order of a Referee Entered in Adversary Proceeding
No. 29. Order and Notice for Final Meeting of Creditors
No. 30. Report of Trustee in No-Asset Case

by combining similar forms, with only minor differences, into one. Consequently the typical set of bankruptcy forms sold by legal stationery businesses might include the following.

1. Instruction Sheet
2. Voluntary Petition
3. Schedules and Others
4. Statement of Affairs
5. Statement of Compensation
6. Creditors List
7. Worksheets, Heavy Duty Envelope, and Covers

The forms come in sets of 4, with the original and two copies to be filed and the remaining form retained for one's personal records. Worksheets are also included. The forms should be filled out by typing, but the court would accept them if clearly printed in ink. Use of the work form should minimize making errors on the final forms, but when typographical errors occur they can be marked out with x's. An honest error of fact would not be subject to severe criticism.

Filing the forms consists of delivering the forms to the court clerk whose office is in the bankruptcy court serving the area. The person filing the forms does not have to personally make the delivery, but can have someone else deliver or he can mail the forms to the court clerk. The filing fee is $50, but this can be paid in installments by filing an appropriate form. Separate signatures are required on the Petition, the Statement of Affairs, and the Oath to Schedules A and B, and these signatures should be notarized.

While the copes may be carbon or photocopies, the signatures and notarization should be original on each copy.

The first of the forms is the Petition for voluntary bankruptcy, a copy of which follows.

In re

{   **BANKRUPTCY NO.**

Bankrupt

Include here all names used by bankrupt within last 6 years.

VOLUNTARY PETITION

1. Petitioner's post-office address is

2. Petitioner has[1]

3. Petitioner is qualified to file this petition and is entitled to the benefits of the Bankruptcy Act as a voluntary bankrupt.

Wherefore petitioner prays for relief as a voluntary bankrupt under the Act.

Signed: ....

     ☐ *Attorney for Petitioner*   ☐ *Petitioner*
     (Petitioner signs if not represented by attorney.)

Address: ....

....

VERIFICATION

State of   County of   **ss.:**

INDIVIDUAL: I   the petitioner named in the foregoing petition, do hereby swear that the statements contained therein are true according to the best of my knowledge, information, and belief.

CORPORATION: I   the[2] do hereby swear that the statements contained therein are true according to the best of my knowledge, information, and belief, and that the filing of this petition on behalf of the corporation has been authorized.

PARTNERSHIP: I   a member — an authorized agent — of the partnership named as petitioner in the foregoing petition, do hereby swear that the statements contained therein are true according to the best of my knowledge, information, and belief, and that the filing of this petition on behalf of the partnership has been authorized.

Subscribed and sworn to before me on

....
           Petitioner

....

....
           Official Character

[1] Insert appropriate allegations — resided [or has had his domicile or has had his principal place of business] within this district for the preceding 6 months [or for a longer portion of the preceding 6 months than in any other district].
[2] Insert president or other officer or an authorized agent of the corporation named as petitioner in the foregoing petition.

OF 1, 4 & 5: Petition for voluntary bankruptcy: verifications   © 1973 BY JULIUS BLUMBERG, INC.,

To fill out the proper District number, refer to Appendix 1. In the block beginning "In re" the bankrupt should include all names used in the last 6 years. A woman married during the period would include her maiden name after her married name. A business man would include the name of his business or partnership. Social Security Number should also be included. Under Item 2, an individual completes by saying that he has resided or had his domicile within the state for the preceding 6 months. This particular form is a combination form which can be used by individual, partner, or corporation by filling in the appropriate line, in this case the one beginning individual. The person should sign in the space "Petitioner" and have the signature notarized.

The second form is Schedule A, which has the following subsections.

Schedule A-1 — Priority debts which have priority over other debts.

Schedule A-2 — Creditors holding security — This would include creditors holding mortgages, conditional sales contracts, or other collateral to secure their debt.

Schedule A-3 — Creditors having unsecured claims without priority — This is the most important schedule, as it should include the bulk of creditors and represent the greatest amount of debt relief.

Older forms also include a Schedule A-4, which refers primarily to checks made payable to the debtor, which were transferred to a creditor but returned unpaid, and Schedule A-5 which refers to co-signed debts. These claims are not segregated on the new forms, but are to be included in Schedule A-1, A-2, or A-3 depending on whether they are priority claims, secured, or unsecured, respectively. Schedule A-1, which lists creditors having priority claims, follows.

The form asks that the debtor "specify when claim was incurred." If an exact date is not known, an approximate date should be indicated. Several

In re

> BANKRUPTCY NO.

Bankrupt

Include here all names used by bankrupt within last 6 years.

Schedule A — STATEMENT OF ALL DEBTS OF BANKRUPT

Schedules A-1, A-2, and A-3 must include all the claims against the bankrupt or his property as of the date of the filing of the petition by or against him.

SCHEDULE A-1 — CREDITORS HAVING PRIORITY

Nature of Claim	Name of creditor and residence or place of business (if unknown, so state); zip codes recommended	Specify when claim was incurred and the consideration therefor; when claim is contingent, unliquidated, disputed, or subject to setoff, evidenced by a judgment, negotiable instrument, or other writing, or incurred as partner or joint contractor, so indicate; specify name of any partner or joint contractor on any debt	Amount of Claim
(a) Wages and commissions owing to workmen, servants, clerks, or traveling or city salesmen on salary or commission basis, whole or part time, whether or not selling exclusively for the bankrupt, not exceeding $600 to each, earned within 3 months before filing of petition.			$
(b) Taxes owing (itemize by type of tax and taxing authority:) (1) To the United States (2) To any State (3) To any other taxing authority			
(c) (1) Debts owing to any person, including the United States entitled to priority by laws of United States (itemized by type) (2) Rent owing to a landlord who is entitled to priority by the laws of any State accrued within three months before filing the petition, for actual use and occupancy.			
		Total	

OF 6: Schedule A-1   © 1970 BY JULIUS BLUMBERG, INC.,

legal terms are used in the form, and some explanation might be helpful.

Across the top, the form asks when a claim was incurred and what "consideration" was received. One of the requirements of contracts, is that a promise will be enforced only when it has been paid for or purchased. In filling out this form, one would list the item of merchandise or what service he received in return for incurring the debt.

A second term "contingent" means that the debt is not yet due and the other party still has something to do before he is entitled to the money.

The term "unliquidated" refers to a debt which exists but is indefinite in amount. The law does not know how much the claim is worth and permits the parties to bargain over the amount. The term "disputed" should be used where there is a disagreement as to whether any money at all is owed.

"Subject to setoff" is a term which is most applicable in the case of bank accounts. If a person has a checking account balance with the same bank at which he has a loan, the bank may put a hold on the funds in the checking account to protect its outstanding loan. The individual who had planned ahead would have used funds from his checking account for consumption or investment in exempt assets.

The form also asks whether the debt is evidenced by a judgment, negotiable instrument, or other writing. A "judgment" is a court decision as to the obligations of the parties to a lawsuit. A negotiable instrument" is a security, such as a note, which may be transferred by endorsing it to a third party.

Schedule A-1 covers priority debts, which are basically:

1. Wages due workmen, not in excess of $600 each earned within 3 months of filing the petition.
2. Taxes owed to:
   a. the United States
   b. state or municipality
3. Other debts having priority by law.
   a. Rent within 3 months of filing petition

Schedule A-2 covers Creditors holding security. In addition to the information requested in Schedule A-1, this schedule also asks for a description of the security and when it was acquired by the creditor. This schedule covers creditors holding a security interest, chattel mortgage, conditional sales contract, or collateral security for any debt. Typically secured loans are those for appliance, auto, furniture and household goods, home improvement loans, and chattel mortgages covering loans made against personal property.

Schedule A-3 covers unsecured debts, which would typically include utility bills, credit card purchases, department store credit, medical bills, personal loans, and food bills. In effect any bill not included in Schedules A-1 and A-2 would be listed in Schedule A-3. An apartment lease should be included, giving the total amount due for the remainder of the lease out marked as unliquidated, since the amount due will depend on whether the apartment can be subleased and at what rate.

Schedule A-2 — Creditors Holding Security

Name of creditor and residence or place of business (if unknown, so state); zip codes recommended	Description of security and date when obtained by creditor	Specify when claim was incurred and the consideration therefor; when claim is contingent, unliquidated, disputed, subject to setoff, evidenced by a judgment, negotiable instrument, or other writing, or incurred as partner or joint contractor, so indicate; specify name of any partner or joint contractor on any debt	Market value		Amount of claim without deduction of value of security	
			$		$	
		Total				

Name of creditor (including last known holder of any negotiable instrument) and residence or place of business (if unknown, so state); zip codes recommended	Specify when claim was incurred and the consideration therefor; when claim is contingent, unliquidated, disputed, subject to setoff, evidenced by a judgment, negotiable instrument, or other writing, or incurred as partner or joint contractor, so indicate; specify name of any partner or joint contractor on any debt	Amount of claim
		$
	Total	

© 1973 BY JULIUS BLUMBERG, INC.,

Schedule B is a list of all assets and is divided into 4 subschedules.

Schedule B-1 — Real Property

Schedule B-2 — Personal Property

Schedule B-3 — Property not otherwise scheduled

Schedule B-4 — Exempt Property

Schedule B-1 covering real estate has been revised in recent years to reflect gross value of real estate rather than net value. The mortgage of a property would be listed in Schedule A-2 and is not deducted from market value in Schedule B-1. The value of real estate should be contained by having the property appraised by a realtor, not by using original purchase price. Schedule B-1 is on the following page.

Schedule B-2 covers holdings of personal property which, for all practical purposes, includes all property which is not classified as real estate. Even if property is claimed as exempt, it still must be listed in Schedule B-2 as well as Schedule B-4. Schedule B-2 lists property in 22 different categories but the average individual can answer "none" to most of these groups. A number of the groups pertain only to businessmen or farmers. A copy of Schedule B-2 follows Schedule B-1.

SCHEDULE B — STATEMENT OF ALL PROPERTY OF BANKRUPT
Schedules B-1, B-2, B-3, and B-4 must include all property of the bankrupt as of the date of the filing of the petition by or against him.
Schedule B-1 — Real Property

Description and location of all real property in which bankrupt has an interest (including equitable and future interests, interests in estates by the entirety, community property, life estates, lease-holds, and rights and powers exercisable for his own benefit)	Nature of interest (specify all deeds and written instruments relating thereto)	Market value of bankrupt's interest without deduction for secured claims listed in schedule A-2 or exemptions claimed in schedule B-4
		$
Total		

Schedule B-2 — Personal Property

Type of Property	Description and location	Market value of bankrupt's interest without deduction for secured claims listed on schedule A-2 or exemptions claimed in schedule B-4
a. Cash on hand		$
b. Deposits of money with banking institutions, savings and loan associations, credit unions, public utility companies, landlords, and others		
c. Household goods, supplies, and furnishings		
d. Books, pictures, and other art objects; stamp, coin, and other collections		
e. Wearing apparel, jewelry, firearms, sports equipment, and other personal possessions		
f. Automobiles, trucks, trailers, and other vehicles		
g. Boats, motors, and their accessories		
	Total	

OF 6: Schedule B-1 & B-2

Schedule B-3 covers property not otherwise scheduled. Primarily, this covers property transfers to creditors within the last 4 months, which subjects them to particular scrutiny of the court. One of the major functions of the bankruptcy proceeding is to review recent transactions between debtor and creditor, to determine if one creditor is getting "preferential" treatment over other creditors of the same class.

Schedule B-4 is to include Property Claimed as Exempt. If the debtor has planned ahead, most of his assets should fall in this category and their values should not exceed the exempt value for those items permitted by the state residence. A summary of state exemptions is covered in Appendix.

Copies of Schedules B-3 and B-4 are on the following two pages.

Schedule B-3 — Property Not Otherwise Scheduled

Type of property	Description and location	Market value of bankrupt's interest without deduction for secured claims listed in schedule A-2 or exemptions claimed in schedule B-4	
a. Property transferred under assignment for benefit of creditors, within 4 months prior to filing of petition (specify date of assignment, name and address of assignee, amount realized therefrom by the assignee, and disposition of proceeds so far as known to bankrupt)		$	
b. Property of any kind not otherwise scheduled			
	Total	$	

Schedule B-4 — Property Claimed as Exempt

Type of property	Location, description, and so far as relevant to the claim of exemption, present use of property	Reference to statute creating the exemption	Value claimed exempt
			$
		Total	

A summary of debts and property then follows, based on the preceding schedules.

SUMMARY OF DEBTS AND PROPERTY
(From the statements of the bankrupt in Schedule A and B)

Schedule	Debts and property	Total
	DEBTS	
A—1/a	Wages having priority	
A—1/b(1)	Taxes owing United States	
A—1/b(2)	Taxes owing States	
A—1/b(3)	Taxes owing other taxing authorities	
A—1/c(1)	Debts having priority by laws of the United States	
A—1/c(2)	Rent having priority under State law	
A—2	Secured claims	
A—3	Unsecured claims without priority	
		Schedule A total
	PROPERTY	
B—1	Real property (total value)	
B—2/a	Cash on hand	
B—2/b	Deposits	
B—2/c	Household goods	
B—2/d	Books, pictures, and collections	
B—2/e	Wearing apparel and personal possessions	
B—2/f	Automobiles and other vehicles	
B—2/g	Boats, motors, and accessories	
B—2/h	Livestock and other animals	
B—2/i	Farming supplies and implements	
B—2/j	Office equipment and supplies	
B—2/k	Machinery, equipment, and supplies used in business	
B—2/l	Inventory	
B—2/m	Other tangible personal property	
B—2/n	Patents and other general intangibles	
B—2/o	Bonds and other instruments	
B—2/p	Other liquidated debts	
B—2/q	Contingent and unliquidated claims	
B—2/r	Interests in insurance policies	
B—2/s	Annuities	
B—2/t	Interests in corporations and unincorporated companies	
B—2/u	Interests in partnerships	
B—2/v	Equitable and future interests, rights, and powers in personality	
B—3/a	Property assigned for benefit of creditors	
B—3/b	Property not otherwise scheduled	
B—4	Property claimed as exempt	
		Schedule B total

Finally an oath to Schedules A and B completes this form. The section beginning "Individual" is completed, and the form is signed and notarized.

OATHS TO SCHEDULES A AND B

State of   County of   ss.:

Individual: I   do hereby swear that I have read the foregoing schedules, consisting of   sheets, and that they are a statement of all my debts and all my property in accordance with the Bankruptcy Act, to the best of my knowledge, information, and belief.

Corporation: I   the [*insert president or other officer or an authorized agent*] of the corporation as bankrupt in this proceeding, do hereby swear that I have read the foregoing schedules, consisting of   sheets, and that they are a statement of all the debts and all the property of the corporation in accordance with the Bankruptcy Act, to the best of my knowledge, information, and belief.

Partnership: I   a [*insert member or an authorized agent*] of the partnership named as bankrupt in this proceeding, do hereby swear that I have read the foregoing schedules, consisting of   sheets, and that they are a statement of all the debts and all the property of the partnership in accordance with the Bankruptcy Act, to the best of my knowledge, information, and belief.

Signed:..

Subscribed and sworn to before me on

....

....

official character

In the opinion of the bankrupt-debtor the net value of the non-exempt assets will not exceed $150.00.
(Massachusetts District requires this statement, if applicable. Other Districts may require this or similar statements.)

....

OF 6: Summary of debts & property: oaths   (*To be signed if applicable*)
© 1973 BY JULIUS BLUMBERG, INC..

The second major form is the "Statement of Affairs", which has comprehensive instructions for completing. The name must coincide with that on the Petition. A number of the questions are intended to eliminate the possibility of fraudulent transfers of property or preferential treatment of one creditor over another. If bankruptcy has been prepared for properly, no loan should have been repaid in the last 4 months as it might be considered preferential treatment. In the case of any loan repaid in the last 12 months, the debtor must be able to prove that the loan was made in good faith and for fair consideration. The Statement of Affairs must be signed and notarized.

UNITED STATES DISTRICT COURT FOR THE _____ DISTRICT OF _____

In re

_____ Bankrupt

Include here all names used by bankrupt within last 6 years.

BANKRUPTCY NO.

STATEMENT OF AFFAIRS
FOR BANKRUPT
NOT ENGAGED IN BUSINESS

Each question should be answered or the failure to answer explained. If the answer is "none," this should be stated. If additional space is needed for the answer to any question, a separate sheet, properly identified, and made a part hereof, should be used and attached.

The term "original petition," as used in the following questions, shall mean the petition filed under Bankruptcy Rule 103, 104 or 106.

1. Name and residence.

a. What is your full name and social security number?

b. Have you used, or been known by, any other names within the 6 years immediately preceding the filing of the original petition herein?
(If so, give particulars.)

c. Where do you now reside?

d. Where else have you resided during the 6 years immediately preceding the filing of the original petition herein?

2. Occupation and income.

a. What is your occupation?

b. Where are you now employed?
(Give the name and address of your employer, or the address at which you carry on your trade or profession, and the length of time you have been so employed.)

c. Have you been in a partnership with anyone, or engaged in any business during the 6 years immediately preceding the filing of the original petition herein?
(If so, give particulars, including names, dates, and places.)

d. What amount of income have you received from your trade or profession during each of the 2 calendar years immediately preceding the filing of the original petition herein?

e. What amount of income have you received from other sources during each of these 2 years?
(Give particulars, including each source, and the amount received therefrom.)

3. Tax returns and refunds.

a. Where did you file your last federal and state income tax returns for the 2 years immediately preceding the filing of the original petition herein?

b. What tax refunds (income and other) have you received during the year immediately preceding the filing of the original petition herein?

c. To what tax refunds (income or other), if any, are you, or may you be, entitled?
(Give particulars, including information as to any refund payable jointly to you and your spouse or any other person.)

4. Bank accounts and safe deposit boxes.

a. What bank accounts have you maintained alone or together with any other person, and in your own or any other name within the 2 years immediately preceding the filing of the original petition herein?
(Give the name and address of each bank, the name in which the deposit was maintained, and the name and address of every other person authorized to make withdrawals from such account.)

b. What safe deposit box or boxes or other depository or depositories have you kept or used for your securities, cash, or other valuables within the 2 years immediately preceding the filing of the original petition herein?
(Give the name and address of the bank or other depository, the name in which each box or other depository was kept, the name and address of every other person who had the right of access thereto, a brief description of the contents thereof, and, if the box has been surrendered, state when surrendered, or, if transferred, when transferred, and the name and address of the transferee.)

5. Books and records.

a. Have you kept books of account or records relating to your affairs within the 2 years immediately preceding the filing of the original petition herein?

b. In whose possession are these books or records?
(Give names and addresses.)

c. If any of these books or records are not available, explain.

d. Have any books of account or records relating to your affairs been destroyed, lost or otherwise disposed of within the 2 years immediately preceding the filing of the original petition herein?
(If so, give particulars, including date of destruction, loss, or disposition, and reason therefor.)

6. Property held for another person.

What property do you hold for any other person?
(Give name and address of each person, and describe the property, or value thereof, and all writings relating thereto.)

7. Prior bankruptcy.

What proceedings under the Bankruptcy Act have previously been brought by or against you?
(State the location of the bankruptcy court, the nature and number of each proceeding, the date when it was filed, and whether a discharge was granted or refused, the proceeding was dismissed, or a composition, arrangement, or plan was confirmed.)

8. Receiverships, general assignments, and other modes of liquidation.

a. Was any of your property, at the time of the filing of the original petition herein, in the hands of a receiver, trustee, or other liquidating agent?
(If so, give a brief description of the property, the name and address of the receiver, trustee, or other agent, and, if the agent was appointed in a court proceeding, the name and location of the court and the nature of the proceeding.)

b. Have you made any assignment of your property for the benefit of your creditors, or any general settlement with your creditors, within one year immediately preceding the filing of the original petition herein?
(If so, give dates, the name and address of the assignee, and a brief statement of the terms of assignment or settlement.)

9. Property in hands of third person.

Is any other person holding anything of value in which you have an interest?
(Give name and address, location and description of the property, and circumstances of the holding.)

10. Suits, executions, and attachments.

a. Were you a party to any suit pending at the time of the filing of the original petition herein?
(If so, give the name and location of the court and the title and nature of the proceeding.)

b. Were you a party to any suit terminated within the year immediately preceding the filing of the original petition herein?
(If so, give the name and location of the court, the title and nature of the proceeding, and the result.)

c. Has any of your property been attached, garnished, or seized under any legal or equitable process within the 4 months immediately preceding the filing of the original petition herein?
(If so, describe the property seized or person garnished, and at whose suit.)

11. Loans repaid.

What repayments on loans in whole or in part have you made during the year immediately preceding the filing of the original petition herein?
(Give the name and address of the lender, the amount of the loan and when received, the amounts and dates of payments and, if the lender is a relative, the relationship.)

12. Transfers of property.

a. Have you made any gifts, other than ordinary and usual presents to family members and charitable donations, during the year immediately preceding the filing of the original petition herein?
(If so, give names and addresses of donees and dates, description, and value of gifts.)

b. Have you made any other transfer, absolute or for the purpose of security, or any other disposition, of real or tangible personal property during the year immediately and preceding the filing of the original petition herein?
(Give a description of the property, the date of the transfer or disposition, to whom transferred or how disposed of, and, if the transferee is a relative, the relationship, the consideration, if any, received therefor, and the disposition of such consideration.)

13. Repossessions and returns.

Has any property been returned to, or repossessed by, the seller or by a secured party during the year immediately preceding the filing of the original petition herein?
(If so, give particulars including the name and address of the party getting the property and its description and value.)

14. Losses.

a. Have you suffered any losses from fire, theft, or gambling during the year immediately preceding or since the filing of the original petition herein?
(If so, give particulars, including dates, names, and places, and the amounts of money or value and general description of property lost.)

b. Was the loss covered in whole or part by insurance?
(If so, give particulars.)

15. Payments or transfers to attorneys.

a. Have you consulted an attorney during the year immediately preceding or since the filing of the original petition herein?
(Give date, name, and address.)

b. Have you during the year immediately preceding or since the filing of the original petition herein paid any money or transferred any property to the attorney or to any other person on his behalf?
(If so, give particulars, including amount paid or value of property transferred and date of payment or transfer.)

c. Have you, either during the year immediately preceding or since the filing of the original petition herein, agreed to pay any money or transfer any property to an attorney at law, or to any other person on his behalf?
(If so, give particulars, including amount and terms of obligation.)

State of   County of   ss.:

I,   do hereby swear that I have read the answers contained in the foregoing statement of affairs and that they are true and complete to the best of my knowledge, information, and belief.

Subscribed and sworn to before me on

Bankrupt

Official character

A complete set of usable forms for Personal Bankruptcy is available and may be ordered by using the form at the back of this book.

Bankruptcy And The Businessman

The problem of bankruptcy for a giant, complex business is obviously one beyond the scope of this book. However, for the small businessman operating a proprietorship, or even a small partnership, the process of bankruptcy may be little different than personal bankruptcy. In this chapter, we cover the following three major areas:

1. Some differences in procedures and forms for the businessman declaring bankruptcy.
2. Scope and magnitude of business bankruptcies today.
3. The danger of accelerating bankruptcies in the years ahead and how the businessman can minimize his exposure.

Differences in Forms and Procedures

Much of the difference between personal and business bankruptcies is due to the larger size of the average business bankruptcy, which makes it more time consuming, complex, and expensive. In the Brookings study on bankruptcy, mentioned earlier, the average time for a business bankruptcy case was 23 months, almost twice that of a personal bankruptcy case. In business cases priority creditors received 36% of the amounts proved and allowed, whereas in personal bankruptcies the comparable figure was only 13%. In business cases secured creditors received 31% of amounts proved and allowed, whereas the comparable figure for personal bankruptcies was only 8%. In both personal and business, the unsecured creditors averaged less than 10% of amounts proved and allowed. The amounts would have been even a lower percentage, except many creditors did not even bother to prove their claims. The median scheduled assets in business cases were $12,000 but only about $3,000 of this was collected. In contrast, median debts were $40,000.

A second major difference between business bankruptcies and personal bankruptcies arises when the business is incorporated. In my book "How To Form Your Own Corporation Without A Lawyer For Under $50", I discuss the advantages and disadvantages of incorporating. As pointed out there, one of the corporation's major advantages is that the personal liability to the founder is limited to the amount of money put into the corporation, with the exception of unpaid taxes. In contrast, in a proprietorship or partnership, the owners are personally liable for all debts and judgments against the business, including liability in case of failure or other disaster. In a partnership each member can bind the other so that one partner can cause the other to be personally liable. Because a corporation by definition has limited liability, it is not important that a corporation receive a discharge from debts unless it intends to stay in business. In contrast discharge from debts is the crucial objective in declaring personal bankruptcy.

Technically, those corporations attempting to stay in business under the protection of our bankruptcy laws are not asking to be declared bankrupt, but are petitioning for reorganization under the various chapters of the bankruptcy law. The National Bankruptcy Act as amended in 1938 provided under Chapter 11, a distinct procedure to simplify reorganization of small corporations. Chapter 11 proceedings are not available to a debtor when there are publicly held securities or when the corporation needs a thorough reorganization. In the latter case, the corporation seeking relief must file under Chapter 10 of the Act.

Chapter 11 is similar in many respects to the Chapter 13 Wage Earner Plan, but is restricted to corporations. It is an "arrangement" which provides a plan for settlement, satisfaction, or extension of time of payment of unsecured debts. It may include:

1. Provisions for treatment of unsecured debts or a parity with each other, or for the divisions of debts into different classes to receive different treatment.
2. Provision for rejection of executory contract.
3. Provision for specific undertakings by debtor, including provision for payments on account.
4. Provision for termination.
5. Provision for continuation of debtor's business, with or without supervision.
6. Provision for payment of debts incurred after filing of petition.
7. Provision for retention of jurisdiction of the court until provisions of the arrangement have been performed.

While much of the publicity about business bankruptcies refers to Chapter 10 and Chapter 11 cases, most small businesses file for straight bankruptcy. (In the Brookings study this was true of 90%).

The straight bankruptcy procedure is the same for business as it is for personal bankruptcies, starting with the petition. Creditors are more likely to show up for the First Meeting of Creditors but tend to be inactive. The

Brookings study pointed out that restraining orders were almost never needed in personal bankruptcy cases, but were requested in 24% of the business cases to prevent creditors from trying to collect before the proceeding was finished.

A partnership is considered a separate legal entity in bankruptcy proceedings separate and distinct from its members. It may be adjudged a bankrupt without the individual partners being adjudged, or it may be adjudged bankrupt along with one or more of the general partners. If a petition is filed on behalf of a partnership by less than all of the general partners, it must allege that the partnership is insolvent. The partnership property must first be applied to partnership debts and property of the individual partners first applied to their individual debts. Any surplus of any partner after paying individual debts is applied to the partnership debts, and vice versa. In the event that one or more but not all of the partners are adjudged bankrupts, the partnership property cannot be administered in bankruptcy except with the consent of the general partners not adjudged bankrupt. However, the latter must settle the partnership business as quickly as possible.

In the case of corporations, the directors of a corporation have the power to file a petition in voluntary bankruptcy. In some states, however, they may require authorization of stockholders. An officer of the corporation, in order to file a bankruptcy petition, would have to be given this authority by the directors.

The Statement of Affairs for business includes most of what is included in that for bankrupts not engaged in business, but requests additional information as follows:

1. Nature and location of business.
2. Financial statements.

3. Inventories.

4. Income other than from operations of business.

5. Accounts and other Receivables.

6. Business Leases.

7. Withdrawals.

8. Members of partnership: officers, directors, managers and principal stockholders of corporation.

A complete Statement of Affairs for Bankrupts with comprehensive instructions for completing for those engaged in business is included in Appendix.

Scope and Magnitude of Business Bankruptcies Today

The rate of business failure has always been high, even in favorable economic times. This is not apparent from bankruptcy figures, since many companies go out of business by selling out to others, filing for reorganization, or just closing down.

The economy in the last decade has been far from favorable, as inflationary pressures became uncontrollable. Our economy has suffered an inflationary bias since the 1930's but high rates of inflation have been concentrated in or after periods of war. The recent burst of inflation has been attributed to President Johnson's "guns and butter" decisions, which superimposed expenditures for "Great Society" programs upon the already high level of government expenditures for the "Vietnam War". Nor has the Federal Government been the only governmental body contributing to inflation. State and local government expenditures were less than 6% of Gross National Product in 1947 but increased to 8% in 1957, 11% in 1967, and currently are running at 14% in 1975. Altogether total government spending has increased from 9% of National Income to 40% in the last 40 years. Government also contributed directly to reported inflation by imposition of various so-called consumer protection and pollution control legislation that diverted substantial amounts of capital expenditures by the private sector of the economy into non-productive uses.

The government's response to inflationary pressures was to try to control the symptoms, not the causes, by various measures including price controls.

The industries hurt first were those most under government controls. The regulated industries, such as the electric utilities, were unable to raise prices nearly as fast as costs rose. While regulators were reluctant to permit the necessary price increases needed to finance the growth of the industry, they did encourage less conservative accounting that made earnings look larger. This did not produce additional cash flow, however, and the utilities had to increase borrowing. Eventually, the safety of their bonds and stocks deteriorated, so that this vital industry was threatened with stagnation.

The defense industry was another victim of the economy. Many, if not most, of the defense companies had contracts with only limited protection against inflation. In the case of new technological products, it was extremely difficult to forecast the cost, particularly when contracts were subject to frequent modification by the military. As costs skyrocketed largely due to unexpectedly high rates of inflation, defense companies incurred substantial losses. Highly vocal opponents of the war were highly critical of any aid to the defense companies, and many could have gone bankrupt if these critics had prevailed. Lockheed is the most famous near-victim which was rescued only by special government action. However, the problem was very widespread and numerous smaller companies, particularly in the military electronics field, disappeared.

Some industries were able to raise prices, but this was no guarantee of survival in an inflationary economy. One of the most uncontrolled areas of inflation was the real estate industry where cost and prices rose much faster than the economy. During the early 1970's billions of dollars, much of it speculative, flowed into Real Estate Investment Trusts which were created to finance the building industry. Unfortunately, the demand for most products diminishes as the price rises rapidly, so that the industry became overbuilt and unprofitable. Many leaders of the industry are near bankruptcy, kept alive by the banks which have made substantial loans to them and hate to see those loans become worthless. One of the largest companies in the industry recently reported that non-earning assets and foreclosed properties had increased to $448 million, or 94% of Total Loans and Investments!

Eventually the spreading economic chaos hit the consumer directly, partly by increasing unemployment and partly by reducing real income. Those industries unable to earn a satisfactory rate of return were unable to expand, so that shortages became widespread. The frustrated consumer found his basic necessities of life going up faster than his income, as food shortages raised food prices, cost of gasoline and utilities rose, and dwelling costs rose sharply. Consumer oriented companies found themselves in financial trouble along with the rest of the economy. In the early 1970's Chrysler was rumored to be in serious financial troubles. More recently W. T. Grant, one of the country's large retail chains, has filed for protection under the Bankruptcy Act.

In looking at these individual bankruptcies, we must remember that they represent only the tip of an iceberg. A W. T. Grant has many suppliers who will feel the impact of the company's bankruptcy. Similarly, a bankruptcy by New York City would spread financial troubles broadly across the nation. To use an isolated example, the common stock of Pullman has recently incurred substantial weakness in the stock market. One analyst's explanation for the weakness was that Pullman has a $200 million contract to deliver 750 mass transit cars to New York City. This analyst feels the company would *only* lose $50 million or about one sixth of its book value, and consequently will survive. But most companies, especially smaller ones, are not as financially strong as Pullman.

Financial problems are so widespread, that the banking structure of the country has been undermined. In the following table we can see the strain on New York City Banks from W. T. Grant, New York City, and the R.E.I.T. industry. Add to this the problem in consumer loans, where the delinquency rate has been running at almost double the level of only a few years ago.

NEW YORK CITY BANKS
EXPOSURE TO MAJOR DEBTOR
DEFAULTS

Company	Total Equity 6/30/75 (millions)	Estimated N.Y.C. Exposure[1] (millions)	W. T. Grant Exposure (millions)	Estimated R. E. I. T. Exposure[1] (millions)
Chase Manhattan	$1,547	300	97	750
Citicorp	2,217	250	97	780
Chemical	761	275	40	720
J. P. Morgan	1,104	225	97	295
Manufacturers	925	225	48	415
Bankers Trust	597	120	32	650

[1]Estimated exposure is taken from report, "The Banking Environment: Certain Concerns", by Goldman Sachs, November 10, 1975.

We do not imply that the debts of New York, W. T. Grant, and the R.E.I.T. industry represent total losses to the banks. On the other hand defaults of the debtors will undoubtedly trigger other loan defaults in a domino effect throughout the economy.

We can only conclude that the threat of bankruptcy is apparently everywhere in our business community.

How Businessmen Can Minimize Exposure To Risk Of Bankruptcy

Today the smart businessman is no longer concentrating his efforts on growing faster than his competitors. For the time being he is concentrating on survival. When his more speculative competitors have collapsed, he will be able to grow by picking up their share of the market.

Survival starts with a strong balance sheet. The credit of a customer is being scrutinized very carefully. The story is told of a salesman who had had a bad day being turned down by customer after customer. Finally, he was pleasantly amazed to be warmly greeted by a customer who bought everything he had to sell. His delight vanished a few days after the goods were shipped, as the customer declared bankruptcy. One is reminded of the advice "if something sounds too good to be true, then it probably isn't."

Inventories are being reduced permitting a reduction of borrowed money used to finance those inventories. An acquaintance who once worked in the inventory control field told me that he used a rule of thumb that it costs 25 cents per annum including interest, storage cost, losses through theft and deterioration, etc., to carry a dollar of inventory. With this much of a handicap, it is easier to lose money than make it by speculating in inventory.

As accounts receivable and inventory are reduced, a company can improve its financial position by either increasing cash or reducing debts with the money formerly tied up in the above areas. Businessmen are also analyzing carefully fixed assets which produce unsatisfactory or no profit and turning these assets into cash.

While the balance sheet is receiving renewed attention, the income statement is not being overlooked. Inflation forces the businessman to become more sophisticated in analyzing the income statement. He has become aware that standard accounting produces mythical profits during inflation. He may buy a product for $10 and sell it at $20, but is there any profit if the same article costs him $20 when he replenishes his inventory. He may not even have sufficient cash to buy the same article at the new price, since Big Government and Big Labor would demand a share in the above profit even though it is more imaginary than real. Similarly depreciation charges against an older machine will be insufficient to provide funds to replace that machine during inflationary periods. Much of the profit reported by our heavy industries would disappear if the costs of depreciation were reported realistically to reflect inflation.

Attempts have been made by financial analysts to adjust corporate earnings for these distortions. The following charts illustrate the wide variance between reported and adjusted earnings. The first chart shows that reported earnings in 1974 were almost triple earnings adjusted to remove the inflationary effect. The second chart shows that manufacturing corporations are earning only 4% on invested capital after the inflation adjustment as compared to a 12% reported rate of return.

NONFINANCIAL CORPORATIONS REPORTED PROFITS FROM ALL SOURCES

Billions of Dollars

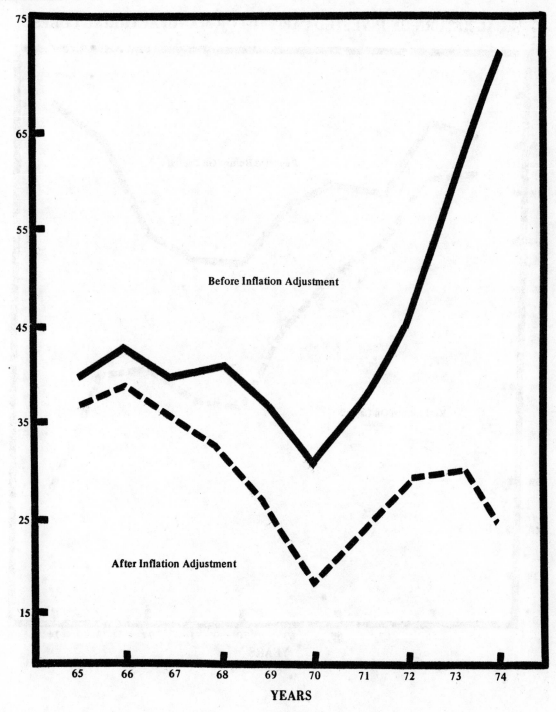

Before Inflation Adjustment

After Inflation Adjustment

YEARS

REAL RETURN ON INVESTED CAPITAL FOR MANUFACTURING CORPS.

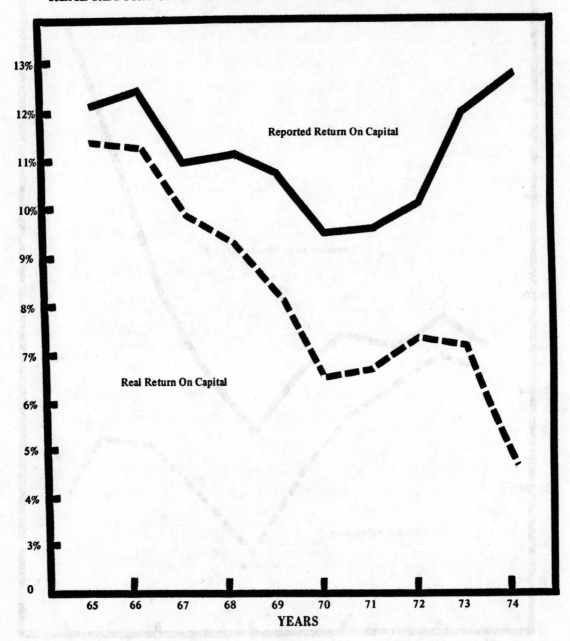

When business fails to earn an adequate return on investment, it can temporarily meet part of its financial needs by drawing down its current assets or increasing its current liabilities, and business has been doing this at a rapid rate. The first of the charts on the following two pages illustrates the decline in cash held by manufacturing corporations, so that this method of meeting the shortfall caused by inadequate earnings is no longer significant. Once excess cash is used up, corporations can also reduce accounts receivables by tightening up credit or can borrow more heavily themselves from the banks or trade sources of credit. This process has already gone a long way, as illustrated by the second chart which measures the Quick Ratio, or ratio of cash and accounts receivables to current liabilities.

The chart offers some valuable insight into the reason that inflation and financial problems are closely linked. The businessman may feel very successful in early stages of inflation, as reported earnings look good. He wants to expand, of course, in order to keep up with demand. Unfortunately, his real earnings are much less than reported earnings, so that he has to borrow money to finance his expansion. At some point in the economic cycle the government or Federal Reserve gets disturbed by the rising rate of inflation and attempts to put on the brakes. At this point the businessman can suddenly become very uncomfortable. His customers slow down their spending rate at a time when his costs are reaching peak levels, aggravated by high interest expenses and high depreciation charges from plant or store space that he has recently added at high cost. He becomes a bankruptcy candidate.

For the knowledgeable businessman, however, the period ahead can be one of opportunity as less able competitors fail to adjust to the difficult conditions. As large corporations discontinue low profit margin business, the small business may be able to move into that area, and, with his lower overhead, make a good profit on it. In such cases he may be able to obtain

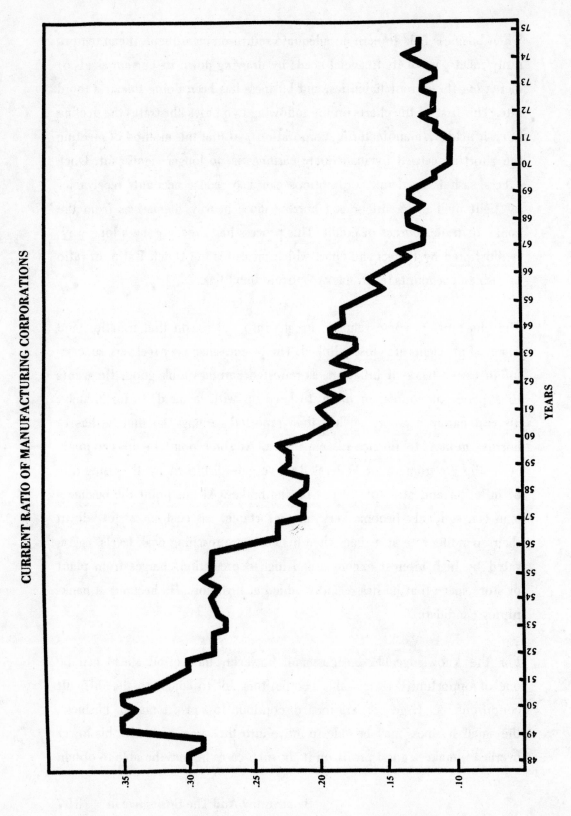

CURRENT RATIO OF MANUFACTURING CORPORATIONS

YEARS

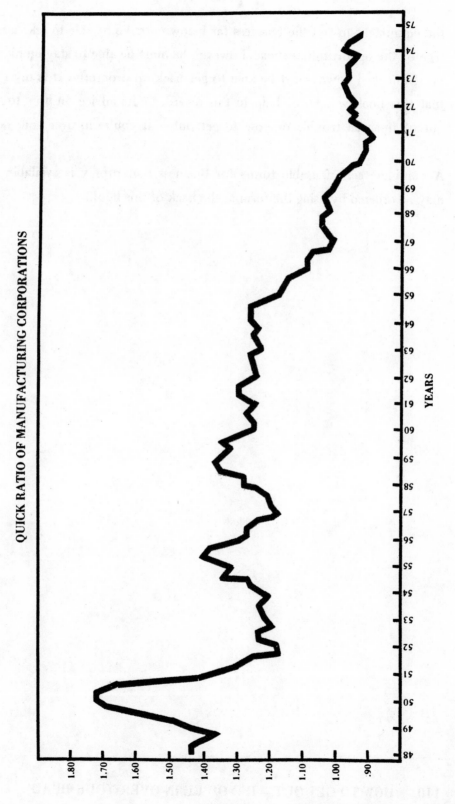

QUICK RATIO OF MANUFACTURING CORPORATIONS

YEARS

the equipment to run the business far below cost. To be able to take advantage of the opportunities ahead, however, he must be able to stay on his feet or, if knocked down, must be able to get back up promptly. It is my hope that this book will be of help in this regard, by its advice on how to stay out of financial trouble or how to get out — if you're in over your head.

A complete set of usable forms for Business Bankruptcy is available and may be ordered by using the form at the back of this book.

A Final Note

How Americans Are Adapting To The Inflation-Recession Economy

The inflation-recession economy which has accelerated in intensity in recent years is in the process of producing widespread changes in American society. One long term trend has been a substantial decline in the size of the American family. While this decline has been attributed to a number of factors, including highly publicized dangers of overpopulation, a simpler explanation may be that children are an expensive investment. With smaller families, people can live comfortably in smaller houses, drive smaller cars, spend less on education, etc. In the case of younger families, the wife can work longer before having children, so that the family has two wage earners during the early part of the marriage when expenses of establishing the household are unusually heavy.

On a shorter term basis we see a major change taking place in higher education. A few years ago the in thing in college was to major in glamorous new fields such as marine biology or highly academic subjects such as medieval history. In each case 100 students might be preparing for a career where only 1 job opening was likely to exist. A student preparing for what was considered to be a dull job in the business world was likely to experience disrespect if not scorn from his fellow students and professors with their more lofty viewpoints. In contrast a swing has now been taking place back toward practical education. The fastest growing field of higher education has been the two year college programs stressing job related courses. Particularly important is the growth in the para-professional areas, such as dental and medical technicians. A major phenomenon of recent years has been the fact that the service area of the economy has been growing much faster than the agricultural and manufacturing areas. Service businesses account for 50 percent of consumer dollars and it is growing each year. The productivity of lawyers, doctors, dentists, engineers, etc., can greatly be increased by intelligent use of para-professionals to handle the more routine work and this trend is accelerating.

In the employment area we see mixed trends developing. The job seeker has a much more difficult task than formerly. Many companies will deteriorate in the more difficult economy we now live in. If employed by such a firm, he will have neither job security nor opportunity.

It has been a common experience in the post war period for a college graduate to get a salary increase each year but find that this increase may leave him only even with what the new college graduate earns. During periods of economic prosperity, this is an encouragement to changing jobs often, but it becomes more risky during periods of high unemployment.

We would expect the most successful families to have multiple sources of income. Partly this will consist of the wife working even when she has had children. In Scandinavian countries where socialism has reached an advanced stage, a wife who doesn't work is sometimes referred to as a "luxury wife". The main wage earner of the family is also likely to have a second part time job, as has been true of many industrious Americans for years.

In our opinion the opportunity for small part time businesses is and will continue to be great. Some of those businesses started part time will eventually become large thriving enterprises. Larger companies are already over-burdened with government regulation, making it difficult to take advantage of new opportunities that arise. Caught in a profit squeeze, large companies will even be divesting themselves of certain businesses which earn little or no profit and unrelated to their main business lines. These can be great opportunities for the alert entrepreneur. Often the small business man can make a good profit in these areas just by having lower overhead and greater flexibility in controlling his costs.

Many Americans have had a kind of supplemental part time business for years, although they may not have realized it. They are "do-it-yourselfers". The main source of wealth accumulated by average Americans over the years has been their homes. Partly this has been due to inflation of real estate values, but a great deal has been due to home improvements and/or home maintenance done by the individuals themselves. In the last few years of escalating food prices, many families are also rediscovering the art of gardening. Maintaining and repairing the family car has long been a favorite pastime of many Americans.

An interesting variation of the do-it-yourselfers is the bartering of services between others who have different skills. One person may be an amateur photographer and another may be a do-it-yourself carpenter. If each were to sell their product to the other, the proceeds from their efforts would be taxable. Technically, the bartering of services probably also produces taxable income, particularly if the exchange is between strangers. However, every day millions of Americans exchange favors with each other and even the most aggressive tax collector would probably not attempt to tax these transactions. An acquaintance tells me of the financial difficulty one of his employees had when she left a small Virginia town to take a better paying job in a medium sized city. In her small home town, her grandfather was a farmer, her father a retailer, her uncle a doctor, her cousin an auto mechanic, etc. Regardless of what she needed in her home town, she was able to obtain it at a discount or free. She in turn had had certain skills with which she had been able to help the others. In her new job she didn't have these opportunities even with a higher income.

Not only are Americans learning to tap new sources of income, they are also becoming sharper consumers. They seek bargains and various creative ways to cut buying costs. When a person gets into the 50% tax bracket, a penny saved is equivalent to two cents earned.

Some Americans are becoming aware that the sole fundamental cause of inflation is the government. Through deficit spending and the pumping of more dollars into the money supply the inevitable result is double digit inflation, with the imminent threat and danger in the U.S. of runaway inflation and eonomic collapse. This writer has spoken to survivors of Germany's inflation and collapse of the mark in the 1920's. All of them preferred living through the war under Hitler to the horror of the collapse of the currency with the inherent problems of shortages and chaos.

The government, like an individual, cannot violate economic axioms with immunity. Government officials spend more than our tax money contributions, most of it in a horrendously irresponsible manner. Then it cannot pay its bills because income is less than outgo. However, the government, unlike the people, has the power to print money. It merely prints more of it thus deficit spending and national debt.

The United States was the founding father of individual rights and its economic consequence — free enterprise. Because of this we experienced in the last 200 years the greatest economic progress and highest living standard the world has ever known. Free enterprise not only is the most moral economic system because it's consistent with man's nature — IT WORKS. Better than any system ever devised. The country's very foundations are unfortunately being threatened by politicians who do not understand free enterprise and are spending us into national bankruptcy.

Our schools are teaching our young people that the free enterprise system does not work, that businessmen are evil, that the government can solve our problems, and that socially conscious jobs, i.e., a welfare worker, are more "noble" than a business career.

I submit that if one wishes to help his fellow man and has some guts, the best way is by starting one's own business, whose by-product is the creation of jobs. That's the best way to help any free individual. Fortunately, there are a few pro-freedom individuals and businessmen. Hopefully enough influence can be exercised by these people to persuade sufficient numbers of Americans as to the dangers of current policies. The only solution, as I see it, is taking steps toward reducing the size and power of government and the elimination of all laws that affect the market place; for there is only one objective regulation of free markets — the law of supply and demand. The result would be not only fewer bankruptcies but unprecedented material progress for us all.

116

ORDER INFORMATION FORM

You can purchase a complete "kit" of usable Wage Earner and Bankruptcy forms for review and consideration depending on your interest. This "kit" contains all forms for:

> **Wage Earner Plan**......$4.95
>
> **Personal Bankruptcy**...$4.95
>
> **Business Bankruptcy**...$4.95
>
> **Total**..............._____

These forms are available from:

> **Enterprise Publishing Co.**
>
> **1300 Market St., Dept. BK**
>
> **Wilmington, DE 19801**

To order, complete this order form and send to the above address along with your check or money order.

NAME _____

ADDRESS _____

CITY _____ STATE _____ ZIP _____

I enclose $_____ check or money order for the following kit(s):

_____ , _____ , _____

_____ .

Glossary

Accommodation — Putting one's name on a note without any consideration or personal benefit, with the intention of lending one's own credit to that of the party accommodated.

Adjudge, Adjudication — An order declaring that the petitioner is bankrupt. When a voluntary petition in bankruptcy is filed, the petitioner automatically becomes adjudicated a bankrupt, eliminating the requirement that the court sign an order to that effect.

Arrangement — An agreement between debtor and creditors for extended payment and/or reduction of all or some of the debts affected by the proceeding.

Attachment — Taking property into legal custody at the initiation of a lawsuit as security for payment of any judgment.

Bankruptcy — Proceedings undertaken in a federal court when a debtor is unable to pay his debts or to reach an agreement with his creditors outside of court.

Chapter (of bankruptcy law) — The Bankruptcy Act of 1938 codified bankruptcy legislation passed by Congress up to that time. Chapters I through VII concerned bankruptcy in general, which contemplates a liquidation of the debtor's assets for the benefit of creditors. Chapter VIII concerns railroad organizations. Chapter IX concerns Municipalities. Chapter X concerns corporate reorganizations which are relatively complex, with Chapter XI providing a simplified procedure called an Arrangement. Chapter XII provides a procedure for Real Property Arrangements, and Chapter XIII covers the Wage Earner Plans.

Chattel Mortgage — A written instrument by which the owner transfers conditional title to personal property to secure the payment of a debt or other obligation.

Composition — An agreement between debtor and creditors in which the creditors agree to accept less than the full amount of their claim. Payments may be made either in lump sum or over a period of time.

Conditional Sales Contract — An agreement to pay a debt secured by the merchandise purchased.

Confirmation — The referee's approval of the debtor's proposed payment plan.

Consideration — Whatever is paid to one person in order to acquire property, money, or other services from another. It may be money or property, but could be a promise to perform or not to perform an act.

Contingent — Possible, but dependent upon the occurrence of some future event which is uncertain or questionable.

Conveyance — A transfer of property by a written document, such as a deed in the case of real property.

Deficiency Judgment — A judgment that creditors can obtain when the proceeds from the sale of collateral is insufficient to pay a secured debt.

Discharge — The release of a debtor from paying the balances of his debts after nonexempt assets are distributed. Does not eliminate debts which are nondischargeable under the Bankruptcy Act.

Encumbrance — A claim against property.

Equity — The value of a property over and above what is owed on it.

Executory Contract — An agreement to perform some action in the future.

Exempt Assets — Property which a bankrupt may keep, being unavailable for satisfying creditor's claims because of federal or state laws applying to bankruptcy proceedings.

Extension — A payment plan that provides for full payment of creditor's claims, but over a longer period of time.

Fraudulent Conveyance — The transfer of his property by a debtor, understandingly and deliberately, to defraud, hinder, or delay his creditors.

Garnishment — Attachment of a person's wages, part of which are paid direct from employer to creditor.

Homestead Exemption Laws — Those statutes which allow a family head to designate a house and land as his homestead, giving it protection against seizure to satisfy general debts.

Insolvency — Usually means inability to pay debts as they come due. Under the Bankruptcy Act, it is usually considered to mean that a Debtor's property is less than his debts.

Judgment — A decision by a court as to the obligations of the parties to a lawsuit.

Levy — Seize property or funds to satisfy a judgment.

Lien — A creditor's interest in property which can then be used for the repayment of an obligation if the debtor defaults.

Negotiable Instrument — A note which can be transferred by endorsing it. To be negotiable an instrument must be signed, be in writing, must contain an unconditional promise to pay a certain amount of money on demand or at some fixed future date.

Note — A written promise to pay a specific amount to a specified person.

Preferential Payment — A transfer of property or money to one creditor which would give him a greater percentage of his debt than other creditors of the same class.

Priority Creditor — A creditor whose claim is in the categories specified by the Bankruptcy Act to be paid first after secured claims and expenses of administering the case have been paid.

Proof of Claim — Formal establishment of a claim by written document. It provides details of amounts owed by bankrupt and the transactions upon which the claim is based.

Referee — The Federal official appointed to preside over bankruptcy cases, similar to a judge in other legal proceedings.

Replevin — Recovery of goods by legal process.

Restraining Order — An injunction (prohibition) by the court preventing a party from proceeding further, with specified actions. In the case of bankruptcy, creditors would be prohibited from maintenance of lawsuits to collect debts.

Schedules — The petitioner's list of debts and assets which are required to be filed with or shortly after the petition.

Secured Creditor — A creditor who holds an interest in collateral as security for the payment of its debt.

Trustee (in bankruptcy) — A person elected by creditors at meeting held before referee or one appointed by referee to collect and distribute property of the bankrupt.

Unliquidated — Not definite in amount.

Usury — Interest charged on a loan which is in excess of that allowed by law.

Bibliography

Books and Pamphlets

Better Business Bureau, *Consumer's Buying Guide,* Universal Publishing and Distributing Co., 1969.

Bogen, Jules I., Editor, *Financial Handbook,* The Ronald Press, 1965.

Burger, Robert E. and Slavlicek, Jan J., *The Layman's Guide to Bankruptcy,* Van Nostrand Reinhold Co., 1971.

Carr, Joseph, *The Power of Money Management,* Financial Publishers, 1967.

Drucker, Peter F., *The Age of Discontinuity,* Harper & Row, 1969.

Faulkner, Harold Underwood, *American Economic History,* Harper & Brothers, 1954.

Foulke, Roy A., *Practical Financial Statement Analysis*, McGraw Hill, 1961.

Groupe, Leonard M., *Going Broke and How To Avoid It*, Thomas Y. Crowell Co., 1972.

Kirk, John, *How To Manage Your Money*, The Benjamin Co., 1966.

Kling, Samuel G., *The Legal Encyclopedia*, Pocket Books, Inc., 1965.

Meyers, Jerome I., *Wipe Out Your Debts & Make A Fresh Start*, Chancellor Press, Inc., 1973.

Nicholas, Ted, *How To Form Your Own Corporation Without A Lawyer For Under $50.00*, Enterprise Publishing Co., 1974.

Newlon, Robert W., *Zwanzig's Bankruptcy Practice & Procedures*, The Allen Smith Co., 1954.

Rutberg, Sidney, *Ten Cents On The Dollar Or The Bankruptcy Game*, Simon & Schuster, 1973.

Stanley, David T. & Girth, Marjorie, *Bankruptcy, Problem, Process, Reform*, The Brookings Institution, 1971.

Reference Book

American Jurisprudence New Topic Service, *Rules of Bankruptcy and Official Forms*, Jurisprudence Publishers, 1974.

Newspaper and Other Articles

Goldman, Sachs & Co., *Investment Strategy Highlights,* Various Bimonthly Reports, 1975.

Legg Mason Washington Service, *Corporate Financial Structure and Public Policy – A Question of Equity,* January, 1975.

Santini, Galeazzo, "Letter From Italy – Money Losers Kept On Life Machine," *The Money Manager,* December 1, 1975.

Associated Press, "March Bankruptcies Set Record," *Wilmington Evening Journal,* May 13, 1975.

APPENDICES

APPENDIX 1 — Federal Court Listing — To file a bankruptcy action go to court nearest your residence. Addresses in phone book.

State	District	City
Alabama	Northern	Birmingham
"	Middle	Montgomery
"	Southern	Mobile
Alaska	–	Anchorage
Arizona	–	Phoenix
Arkansas	Eastern	Little Rock
"	Western	Fort Smith
California	Northern	San Francisco
"	Eastern	Sacramento
"	Central	Los Angeles
"	Southern	San Diego
Canal Zone, Panama	–	Ancon
Colorado	–	Denver
Connecticut	–	New Haven
Delaware	–	Wilmington
District of Columbia	–	Washington
Florida	Northern	Tallahassee
"	Middle	Jacksonville
"	Southern	Miami
Georgia	Northern	Atlanta
"	Middle	Macon
"	Southern	Savannah
Guam	–	Agana
Hawaii	–	Honolulu
Idaho	–	Boise
Illinois	Northern	Chicago
"	Eastern	East St. Louis
"	Southern	Peoria
Indiana	Northern	Hammond
"	Southern	Indianapolis
Iowa	Northern	Cedar Rapids
"	Southern	Des Moines
Kansas	–	Wichita
Kentucky	Eastern	Lexington
"	Western	Louisville
Louisiana	Eastern	New Orleans
"	Western	Shreveport
Maine	–	Portland
Maryland	–	Baltimore
Massachusetts	–	Boston
Michigan	Eastern	Detroit
"	Western	Grand Rapids

State	District	City
Minnesota	–	St. Paul
Mississippi	Northern	Oxford
"	Southern	Jackson
Missouri	Eastern	St. Louis
"	Western	Kansas City
Montana	–	Butte
Nebraska	–	Omaha
Nevada	–	Reno & Las Vegas
New Hampshire	–	Concord
New Jersey	–	Trenton
New Mexico	–	Albuquerque
New York	Northern	Utica & Albany
"	Southern	New York City
"	Eastern	Brooklyn
"	Western	Buffalo
North Carolina	Eastern	Raleigh
"	Middle	Greensboro
"	Western	Asheville
North Dakota	–	Fargo & Bismarck
Ohio	Northern	Cleveland
"	Southern	Columbus
Oklahoma	Northern	Tulsa
"	Eastern	Muskogee
"	Western	Oklahoma City
Oregon	–	Portland
Pennsylvania	Eastern	Philadelphia
"	Middle	Scranton
"	Western	Pittsburgh
Puerto Rico	–	San Juan
Rhode Island	–	Providence
South Carolina	–	Columbia
South Dakota	–	Sioux Falls
Tennessee	Eastern	Knoxville
"	Middle	Nashville
"	Western	Memphis
Texas	Northern	Dallas
"	Southern	Houston
"	Eastern	Tyler & Beaumont
"	Western	San Antonio
Utah	–	Salt Lake City
Vermont	–	Burlington
Virgin Islands	–	Charlotte Amalie
Virginia	Eastern	Norfolk
"	Western	Roanoke & Abingdon
Washington	Eastern	Spokane

State	District	City
Washington	Western	Seattle
West Virginia	Northern	Elkins
"	Southern	Charleston
Wisconsin	Eastern	Milwaukee
"	Western	Madison
Wyoming	–	Cheyenne

APPENDIX 2 – Homestead Exemption Information
(Excluded From Bankruptcy)

State	Amount	Who May Claim
Alabama	Area 160 acres. Value $2,000.	Any resident.
Alaska	Area 160 acres in country. ¼ acre in town or city, laid off in blocks or lots. Value not in excess of $12,000 for trailer or mobile home the exemption is $8,000.	Any resident who owns and uses same as his actual abode.
Arizona	In compact body. Residence and land of debtor not to exceed $15,000 in value, mobile home and land on which it is located not to exceed $8,000 in value. Claim for exemption must be filed in office of County Recorder.	Any person 18 or over married or single who resides in state.
Arkansas	In country, not over 160 acres. Value $2,500. Nor less than 80 acres regardless of value. In city, not over one acre and improvements. Same value as country, not to be reduced to less than ¼ acre regardless of value.	Resident married or head of family.
California	By any head of a family, of not exceeding $20,000 cash value, over and above all liens and encumbrances on the property at time of any levy of execution thereon; by any person 65 or older not exceeding $20,000 in cash value. By any other person, of not exceeding $10,000 in actual cash value, over all liens and encumbrances. House trailer or mobile home in which debtor or his family reside to maximum value of $15,000, over liens and encumbrances. Dwelling can include condominium or can be situated on property leased for a period of thirty years or more. Declaration must be recorded with county recorder.	Resident head of family. By any other resident.
Colorado	No limitation on area. House and lots must not exceed $5,000 in value. Moveable structure to the extent of $5,000 if used and occupied as a place of residence by owner. Word "homestead" must be entered on margin of record title.	Householder, head of family
Connecticut	No homestead exemption.	
Delaware	No homestead exemption.	

Reprinted from the *Credit Manual of Commercial Laws,* 1975, National Association of Credit Management, New York, New York.

State	Amount	Who May Claim
District of Columbia	No homestead exemption.	
Florida	160 acres in country, ½ acre in city. No limit on value may be claimed by recording declaration of homestead or after levy and before sale by ratifying officer who is to sell, in writing of claim of homestead. Interest in 98-year lease qualifies for Homestead exemption.	Head of family residing in state.
Georgia	Real estate not to exceed $500 in city or 50 acres in country with improvements, not to exceed $200. Includes specified personal property. Waiver note or written waiver if given contemporaneously with transaction would hold, but a sale or assignment of homestead has priority to ordinary waiver.	Head of family or aged or infirm person or one having care of dependent female of any age.
Hawaii	"One piece of land" and improvements with area up to 1 acre and property owned by head of family or person 65 years or older may not exceed $20,000 when owned by any other person may not exceed $10,000 as determined by assessed valuation.	Housekeeper "having a family."
Idaho	$10,000 where claimant is the head of family; $4,000 for any other person. Exemption is confined to dwelling house and land on which it is situated. Declaration must be executed and recorded.	Family. By any other person.
Illinois	$10,000 in land with buildings, owned or leased, occupied as residence.	Householder having a family.
Indiana	No homestead statute. Real property exempt to $700. In no event, however, to exceed with the personality $1,000 total. Wife can claim one-third of any real state owned by husband.	Resident householder. Where a husband and wife are each conducting a separate and distinct business each may have the full exemption of $1,000.
Iowa	If within city or town plot must not exceed one-half acre, otherwise not more than 40 acres, but if in either case value is less than $500, it may be enlarged to reach that amount. Exceptions: Homestead liable for deficiency remaining after exhausting all other non-exempt property where debt is contracted prior to acquisition of homestead; by written contract stipulating that	Resident, head of family, husband or wife.

State	Amount	Who May Claim
	homestead shall be liable, also, for debts incurred for work done or material furnished exclusively for the improvement of homestead; also, if no survivor or issue, for payment of debts to which it might at that time be subject if it had never been held as a homestead.	
Kansas	160 acres, farm; 1 acre in city, occupied as residence.	Any resident.
Kentucky	$1,000, unless liability existed before purchase of land. Mortgage on homestead, release or waiver must be in writing and signed also by wife and recorded.	Householder.
Louisiana	$4,000 not over 160 acres. Exemption may be waived. Claim must be in writing and recorded in parish where homestead is situated.	Resident with family or other dependents.
Maine	$3,000 if declaration is filed with registry of deeds.	Householder.
Maryland	None.	
Massachusetts	$24,000 in value of land and buildings. Must be established by deed or declaration and recorded. Provisions for family not exceeding $300 in value, and sewing machine not over $200 in value.	Householder who has family.
Michigan	$3,500 in lot, if in city, and not exceeding 40 acres in extent, if in country.	Resident citizen.
Minnesota	80 acres in country, in village or city ½ acre with improvements.	Resident.
Mississippi	$15,000 in value and not exceeding 160 acres if outside city, town or village. Homestead can be house or apartment or condominium. Homestead exemption is denied under certain circumstances where portions of property are rented or used for other commercial purposes.	Citizen householder with family. Husband or wife, widow or widower without a family, or not occupying homestead, if over 60 years of age, who has been an exemptionship.
Missouri	In country, 160 acres, value $1,500. In cities and towns, $1,500 to $3,000, depending on population. Area in cities and towns also depends on population.	Head of family.

State	Amount	Who May Claim
Montana	Not exceeding $7,500 assessed valuation on 320 acres of agricultural land or ¼ acre in city.	Resident head of family. Resident single person over 60 years.
Nebraska	$4,000, consisting of dwelling in which claimant lives and its appurtenances, not over 160 acres in country; 2 adjoining lots in city.	Head of family.
Nevada	$10,000 but does not apply in claim for purchase price, taxes on property or lien of mortgage or deed of trust created by and with the consent of the husband and wife. Declaration of homestead must be recorded with County Recorder. Mortgage or conveyance of homestead property invalid, unless signature of husband and wife be obtained to same and instrument be acknowledged by wife separately and apart from husband.	Any head of family or husband or wife or single person.
New Hampshire	$2,500.	Debtor, wife and children of debtor.
New Jersey	No statutory provisions.	
New Mexico	$10,000.	Husband and wife or widow or widower living with unmarried daughter or minor son or person supporting himself.
New York	Lot of land with buildings not exceeding $200 or to extent of $1,000 owned and occupied as principal residence by a householder or a woman.	Resident householder or woman, principal residence only.
North Carolina	$1,000.	Resident.
North Dakota	In town plot 2 acres and improvements, value $40,000 above liens. Elsewhere, 160 acres and improvements, no limit on value.	Resident head of family.
Ohio	$1,000.	Husband and wife living together, a widow or a widower living with an unmarried daughter or unmarried minor son.

State	Amount	Who May Claim
Oklahoma	160 acres in country, 1 acre in city, not exceeding $5,000 in value, but not less than ¼ acre.	Resident head of family.
Oregon	Not over $7,500 and not exceeding one block in any town or city laid off into blocks and lots; not exceeding 160 acres elsewhere. Mobile home, $3,000. Proceeds of sale exempt for one year if to be used to purchase another homestead.	Resident house-holder.
Pennsylvania	None.	
Rhode Island	None.	
South Carolina	$1,000 and yearly products. Waiver of un-assigned homestead invalid, except by deed or mortgage. No limitation in area.	Head of family.
South Dakota	Sale price must exceed $15,000 over all encumbrances. In city, 1 acre; in country, 160 acres.	Head of family, or in case he fails to claim, any member of the family over 14 years of age.
Tennessee	$1,000.	Resident head of family.
Texas	Homestead for a family, if not in a city, town or village, not more than 200 acres; single person not in a city, town or village not more than 100 acres; for family or single person in a city, town or village lot or lots not to exceed $10,000 in value.	Head of family.
Utah	$4,000 and $1,500 in addition for wife, also $600 additional for each member of the family.	Head of family.
Vermont	The homestead of a natural person consist-ing of a dwelling house, outbuildings and the land used in connection therewith, not exceeding $5,000 in value, and owned and used or kept by such person as a homestead together with the rents, issues, profits and products thereof.	Housekeeper or head of a family.
Virginia	$2,000.	Resident house-holder or head of family.
Washington	Not exceeding $10,000; except that for state of deceased debtor sum may be $15,000 if court so determines. Consists of	Resident head of family.

State	Amount	Who May Claim
	dwelling house with pertinent buildings and land or land with improvements purchased with the intention of building a house and residing therein. May be selected at any time before sale by filing declaration with county auditor. Not exempt from claims of mechanic's, laborer's or materialmen's liens or from mortgages.	
West Virginia	$1,000. Claim to be executed and recorded.	Husbands, parents, or infants of deceased or insane parents.
Wisconsin	$25,000. Consists of dwelling house and its appurtenances. Not exceeding 4 acres and not less than ¼ acre.	Resident.
Wyoming	$4,000. House and lot or lots in city, on farm consisting of any number of acres within the value limitation. Must be occupied by owner or his family. Creditor may bring proceeding if he believes property worth over $2,500. On sale, if it brings less, creditor liable for expenses.	Householder, being head of family and every resident 60 years or over whether head of family or not. Widow, husband or minor child entitled to homestead on death of owner, subject to debts of deceased.

APPENDIX 3 — Personal Property Exemptions

State	Personal Property Amount	Who May Claim	Wages*
Alabama	$1,000 and necessary family clothing, family portraits and books. Personal property in the custody of a trustee in bankruptcy is exempt to the bankrupt and cannot be garnished. Insurance for benefit of wife and children to extent of premium of $1,000 per year.	Any resident	Of laborers or employees residents of the State in an amount equal to 75% of wages. On judgments based on consumer transactions greater of 80% of weekly disposable income or amount by which disposable earnings per week exceed 50 times federal minimum hourly wage.
Alaska	Miscellaneous personal property, furnishings, and utensils to value of $1,200. Tools, implements, etc. to carry on trade or profession to the value of $2,500. Debtor must designate article for which he claims exemption at the time of levy of exemption. No articles are exempt from execution on a judgment recovered for the purchase price of same.	Any resident.	25% of disposable income for week or amount of $114 of weekly income, whichever is less.
Arizona	Property must be designated by debtor. Household goods, artisans' tools, professional man's equipment, various farm implements, and miscellaneous articles. Money received by surviving spouse or child upon life of deceased spouse or parent not exceeding $10,000.	Every family.	One-half of earnings for 30 days prior to levy when necessary for use of family.
California	Numerous necessary articles for their business, trade, calling, profession, etc., up to $2,500 over and above all encumbrances on the property and household furniture and equipment. Motor vehicle to value above encumbrances on the vehicle provided that the value of the vehicle shall not exceed $500, or as set forth in Used Car Guide or if not set forth	Any person. Farmers, mechanics, miners, truckmen, professional men., etc.	Greater of 50% or portion exempt by federal statute of the earnings of the defendant or judgment debtor received for his personal services rendered at any time within thirty days next preceding the levy of attachment or execution. All of such earnings, if necessary for the use of the debtor's family,

*Title III of the Federal Consumer Credit Protection Act exempts from garnishment the greater of 75% of disposable earnings per work week or an amount each week equal to 30 times the Federal minimum hourly wage. The exemption does not apply to support orders or orders of any court of bankruptcy. The statute does not provide that an employee cannot be discharged because his earnings have been subjected to garnishment for *one* indebtedness. State laws providing lesser limitations are superseded by the Federal law.

Reprinted from the *Credit Manual of Commercial Laws,* 1975, National Association of Credit Management, New York, New York.

| State | Personal Property | | Wages |
	Amount	Who May Claim	
Cal. (cont.)	$1,000, house trailer occupied by debtor family to value of $9,500 above all encumbrances on the house trailer. Relocation payments for a period of six months.		residing in this State, and supported in whole or in part by such debtor unless the debts are: (a) Incurred by such debtor, his wife or family, for the common necessaries of life: or (b) Incurred for personal services rendered by any such employee, or former employee, of such debtor.
Colorado	Necessary wearing apparel for each head of family, single person and dependent to the extent of $400 per person; watches, jewelry and articles of adornment of each head of family, single person and dependent $100 per person; library, family pictures and school books of head of family and dependents to the extent of $500, single person to the extent of $200; burial sites; household goods to the extent of $1,000 in value for head of family and $400 for a single person; provisions and fuel on hand for use head of family and dependents to the extent of $300, for a single person $100; every head of family engaged in agriculture, livestock not exceeding $2,000 and horses, mules, carts, machinery not exceeding $1,500, in the case of a single person, $1,000 and $750 respectively; pensions or compensations as a result of service in the Armed Forces; stock in trade, supplies, fixtures, tools of business not exceeding $750; motor vehicle not exceeding $500; library of a professional person not exceeding $750; life insurance policies to the extent of $5,000; house trailer to the extent of $2,500 while occupied as a place of residence by head of the family; aggregate value of all items excepted shall be limited to $12,500.	Single resident or head of family.	Greater of 75% of disposable earnings per week of amount in which disposable earnings exceed 30 times federal minimum hourly wage for debts arising from consumer credit sales. *Head of family* — 70% of earnings due at time of service. *Single person* — 35% of earnings due at time of service.
Connecticut	Certain specific articles such as apparel, household furniture entirely exempt, and other articles up to designated values.	Resident	Greater of 75% of disposable earnings per week up to greater of $65 or amount equal to 40 times Federal mini-

| State | Personal Property | | Wages |
	Amount	Who May Claim	
Conn. (cont.)			mum hourly wage. SUPPORT ORDERS – $25 per week exempt on court order for support of wife and children.
Delaware	Books, pictures, church pew, burial lot, wearing apparel of family, sewing machines, implements of trade not exceeding $75 in New Castle, Sussex counties and $50 in Kent County. General exemption of personal property – New Castle County $200, Kent County $150.	Any resident

Any resident being head of a fmily. | Exemption of 85% of wages. Support orders – 75% of net wages exempt on order for support of one child reduced by 5% for each additional child. |
| District of Columbia | Implements and tools to extent of $200. Household furniture, etc., to value of $300; also certain miscellaneous articles. Wearing apparel. | Resident head of family or householder.

All persons. | Greater of 75% of disposable earnings per week or amount of disposable earnings per week equal to 30 times Federal minimum hourly wage. *Withholding by Garnishee-Employer* – 90% of first $200 of gross wages payable in a month, 80% of gross wages payable in a month in excess of $200 and under $500. Calendar month consists of 4-1/3 workweeks. *Debtor Principal Support of Family* – $200 each month of earnings other than wages of resident or non-resident earning major portion of livelihood in D.C. exempt for two months preceding issuance of writ. *Debtor Not Principal Support of Family* – $60 each month is exempt. Support judgments 50% of gross wages exempt. |
| Florida | Cash surrender value of life insurance policy. Proceeds of the life insurance of person dying within state. Proceeds of disability insurance unless taken out for benefit of creditors. Other articles up to designated value. | Head of family residing in state. | Entire wages of the head of family when wages are due for personal labor or services of such person. Amount exempt is exclusive of payroll deductions for taxes. |
| Georgia | Value $1,600, real or personal or both, set apart by petition. Purchase money debt enforceable against. | Head of family or aged or infirm person or one having care of dependent female of any age. | Greater of 75% of disposable earnings per week or amount by which disposable earn- |

| | **Personal Property** | | |
State	Amount	Who May Claim	Wages
Ga. (cont.)	(Either this exemption or homestead exemption may be claimed but not both.)		ings exceed 30 times the federal minimum hourly wage.
Hawaii	Various specified articles of personal property. (The exemption does not apply, however, to execution on a judgment recovered for the purchase price of such goods as on a foreclosure of a mortgage on the goods.)	Any resident.	95% of first $100, 90% of next $100 and 80% of gross wages in excess of $200 per month or equivalent per week.
Idaho	In addition to homestead, chairs, tables, desks, books, value $200; certain household articles, value $300; wearing apparel, pictures, family portraits, provisions, for 6 months; farming implements, value $300; 4 oxen or horses, or mules and harness, wagon and food for animals for 6 months, tools of mechanic, value $500. Farming utensils not exceeding in value $300; crops $500; motor vehicles not exceeding in value $200 necessary to carry on trade.	Actual resident.	Greater of 75% of disposable earnings for workweek or amount each week equal to 30 times federal minimum hourly wage.
Illinois	Wearing apparel, Bible, school books, family pictures, military pensions for 1 year, $300, plus $700 if head of family with whom he lives.	Any person.	Of wage-earner to extent of $50 ($65 per week for head of family) per week or 85% of gross wages or amounts prescribed by Federal Consumer Protection Act, Title III whichever is greatest but not in excess of $200 per week exempt from garnishment. Includes compensation by commission or profit allowance.
Indiana	Personal property $600. In no event, however, to exceed with the realty $1,000 total. Intangible personal property including choses in action, profits, debts owing and income owing to value of $15.	Head of family residing in state. Where a husband and wife are each conducting a separate & distinct business out of their own individual funds each may claim exemption to the extent of $1,000.	UCCC provides exemption for 75% of disposable earnings per week in excess of 30 times Federal minimum hourly wage. The following provisions have not been repealed by the UCCC and appear to be in conflict with it: Householder exemption not exceeding $25, resident householder $15 per week plus 90% of excess over $15 exempt as to claims arising out of contract, $1,000 maximum. In *Mins v. Consumer Credit Corp.,* (Ind. Sup. Ct., March

	Personal Property		
State	Amount	Who May Claim	Wages
Ind. (cont.)			13, 1974), the court held that statute most beneficial to house-holder would be enforced.
Iowa	Wearing apparel, books, pictures or musical instruments, certain livestock, food for six months, kitchen furniture not to exceed $200. Tools, equipment, books, etc. used in trade or profession, limited number of farm animals. Wearing apparel and trunk to contain same. Proceeds of life insurance.	Resident, head of family. Non-resident or unmarried resident not head of family.	75% of disposable earnings for week or amount by which disposable earnings for week exceed 30 times federal minimum hourly wage, whichever is greater. Maximum amount that can be garnished in any year is $250 for each creditor.
Kansas	Head of household: (1) Furnishing and supplies, including food & clothing for a period of 1 year; (2) one means of conveyance; (3) family burial plot; (4) equipment or other means of production necessary in carrying on a trade, business, occupation or profession not to exceed $5,000. Not head of household: (1) Personal clothing; (2) equipment or other means of production necessary in carrying on a trade, business, occupation or profession not to exceed $2,000.	Resident, head of family. Any resident.	75% of disposable earnings for week or amount by which disposable earnings exceed 30 times Federal minimum hourly wage, whichever is greater. Exemptions inapplicable to support orders.
Kentucky	Many articles, household good, wearing apparel, etc., not to exceed $1,500 in value, mechanic's tools, livestock not to exceed $1,500 in value; one motor vehicle not to exceed $1,500 in value if used by person engaged in farming or who uses vehicle in his employment, library of professional men, etc.	Resident with a family.	Greater of 75% of disposable income per week or amount by which disposable earnings exceed 30 times Federal minimum hourly wage. Exemptions inapplicable to support orders.
Louisiana	Certain articles specified in statute, such as clothing, tools of a trade and other articles.	Householder.	75% of disposable earnings for any week, but not less than $70 per week. Lenders forbidden to use garnishment on loans with interest in excess of 10%.
Maine	Debtor's apparel, household furniture necessary for the family not exceeding $500 in value; radio and one television not exceeding $200 in value; automobile or truck not exceeding $600 in value; family portraits, Bibles and	Resident.	Greater of 75% of disposable earnings for week or amount by which disposable earnings exceed 30 times federal minimum hourly wage. 40 times the hourly wage in con-

State	Personal Property Amount	Who May Claim	Wages
Maine (cont.)	school books in actual use and library not to exceed $150 in value; watch not exceeding $50 in value; wedding ring and engagement ring not exceeding $200 in value; interest in church pew; one cooking stove, iron stove, charcoal not exceeding 12 cords of wood; anthracite coal not exceeding five tons; bituminous coal not exceeding 50 bushels; $50 worth of lumber; heating gas not exceeding $200; farm produce until harvested one barrel of flour, 50 bushels of oats, 50 barrels of potatoes, corn and grain not exceeding 30 bushels; food necessary for family and debtor; tools necessary for his trade or occupation not exceeding $500 in value; one sewing machine, one refrigerator, one washing machine not exceeding $200 in value; a pair of working cattle or mules, two horses not exceeding $400 in value; domestic fowl not exceeding $100 in value; specified farm equipment; boat not exceeding two tons used in fishing business.		sumer transactions. Wages due debtor for wife's or minor child's personal service are exempt.
Maryland	(1) $500 real or personal property now exempt (no more than $200 in cash). (2) Or certain household goods.	Bona fide residents.	Wages — $120 exempt multiplied by the number of weeks in which such wages due were earned or 75% of such wages, whichever is greater. Except that in Caroline, Worcester, Kent and Queen Anne counties exemption for any workweek shall be greater of 75% of wages due or 30 times Federal minimum hourly wage.
Massachusetts	Many articles. Household furniture not exceeding $3,000 in value. Materials and stock necessary for carrying on trade or business, value of $500. Cash savings or deposits not to exceed $80.	Resident.	Wages for personal labor or services exempted from attachment to amount of $125 per week. Exemption of $75 or personal income which is not otherwise exempt by law.
Michigan	As to householders: certain articles, household goods, amounting to $1,000. As to businessmen: tools, imple-	Resident citizen.	Householder with family — 60% exemption with following limitations: On first garnish-

	Personal Property		
State	Amount	Who May Claim	Wages
Mich. (cont.)	ments, stock in trade necessary to carry on business, $1,000. Partners' right in specific partnership property is not subject to attachment or execution except on a claim against the partnership. When partnership debt there is no exemption under the laws.		ment, maximum $50 per week and minimum $30 per week for labor of one week. For more than one week's labor, maximum $90 and minimum $60. As to subsequent garnishments for one week's labor, maximum per week is $60 and minimum $24. For a period of more than 16 days, maximum is $60 and minimum $30. Employee not householder with family — First garnishment 40% exemption, with $50 maximum and $20 minimum. In other cases 30% or $20 maximum and $10 minimum.
Minnesota	Farm machines and implements and livestock produce and standing crops not exceeding $5,000 in value; tools and stock of a trade or business not exceeding $5,000 in value except that the total of all of the above shall not exceed $5,000; clothes, household furniture, etc., not exceeding $3,000 in value; other specific articles; a mobile home, the earnings of a minor child of any debtor by reason of any liability of any such debtor not contracted for the special benefit of said child. Nothing exempt from execution or attachment in action for balance of purchase price thereof.	Resident.	75% of net wages due at time of attachment, garnishment or levy or 8 times the number of business days and paid holidays not greater than 5 per week in the pay period, times the federal minimum hourly wage, whichever is greater. Where debtor has been on relief, exemption for a period of 6 months from date of return to private employment.
Mississippi	Tools, equipment, etc., used in connection with trade or profession; the books of a student, wearing apparel of every person, libraries of all persons, including books, drawings and paintings, not exceeding $1,200 in value and other specified articles. Specified articles of farm equipment animals and produce, plus household and kitchen, not exceeding in value $1,200 and all family portraits.	Any person. Head of a family.	75% of wages or salaries of resident laborer or employee.
Missouri	Head of family: wearing apparel, family books,	Head of family.	Greatest of (1) 75% of workweek earnings, (2)

State	Amount	Who May Claim	Wages
Missouri (cont.)	furniture worth not more than $200, food not more than $200, assorted animals, books tools of the trade or $500 lump sum in lieu of all the above. Non-head of family: wearing apparel and tools of the trade.	Non-head of family.	weekly amount equal to 30 times federal minimum hourly wage.
Montana	Special articles, including household goods, and tools to carry on business. One automobile or truck value of $300. Proceeds of life insurance purchased with premiums not exceeding $500 per year. Professional libraries. Miner entitled to $1,000. Only wearing apparel to unmarried person under 60 years. Non resident not entitled to exemption.	Resident head of family. Resident single person over 60 years.	All wages for 45 days preceding garnishment if necessary for support of family. If debt incurred for gasoline or common necessities then only 50% is exempt.
Nebraska	Personal possessions of debtor and family; necessary wearing apparel of debtor and family; kitchen utensils and household furniture selected by debtor to $1,500; equipment or tools not exceeding $1,500; provisions for debtor and family necessary for 6 months' support; and fuel necessary for 6 months. All articles intended to be exempt shall be chosen by debtor, his agent or legal rep.; pension of soldier and sailor and property purchased therewith $2,000; life insurance on policies not payable to executor or administrator of insured or his beneficiary in an amount paid for by annual premium not exceeding $500.	Head of family.	Greatest of 75% of disposable earnings or amount equal to 30 times Federal minimum hourly wage or 85% of disposable earnings if wage earner is head of family.
Nevada	Private libraries over $500; family fixtures and keepsakes; necessary household goods, appliances and furniture not over $1,000; farm trucks, farm stocks, farm tools, supplies and seed not over $1,500; tools, instruments and materials used to carry on the trade not over $1,500; dwelling of a miner or prospector not over $500; also cars and appliances necessary to carry on mining operations not over $500; mining claim actually worked by bankrupt not over $1,000		The greater of 75% of disposable earnings or the amount by which disposable earnings exceed 30 times the minimum hourly Federal wage law. Exemption does not apply to support orders.

State	Personal Property Amount	Who May Claim	Wages
Nev. (cont.)	one vehicle not over $1,000 if necessary for occupation or profession of debtor; poultry not over $80; fire engines, hooks and ladders and apparatus of fire company; all arms, uniforms required by law to be kept by debtor plus one gun selected by debtor; all court houses, jails and property related thereto; all monies growing out of any life insurance if annual premium paid not over $500; homestead as provided by law; dwelling of judgment debtor occupied as home for himself and family, not over $10,000 in value, if dwelling is not on lands owned by debtor.		
New Hampshire	Household furniture $1,000; wearing apparel and tools in trade to value of $600. Also miscellaneous property set forth in statute.	Debtor.	Wages for labor performed after service of writ; wages for labor performed before service exempt unless action founded on debt on judgment issued by state court. In such case wages equal to 50 times Federal minimum hourly wage are exempt. Special exemption for small loan law debts.
New Jersey	Personal Property, value $1,000, and wearing apparel.	Head of resident family.	Minimum exemption of $48 per week; 90% exemption if earnings are $7,500 per year or less. If earnings are more than $7,500 reduced exemption percentage by order of court.
New Mexico	Wearing apparel, household goods under certain values. Many specified articles. $500 real or personal property exclusive of articles specified if debtor has no homestead, unless debt is for necessaries or for manual labor. Resident not having household has additional exemption of $1,000 of personal property. Personal property used as security under UCC is not exempt.	Resident. There are some minor differences for a non-head of household.	Greater of 75% of debtor's disposable earnings or of excess of 40 times Federal minimum hourly wage rate. Disposable earnings is that part of debtor's salary remaining after deduction of amounts required to be withheld by law.
New York	All wearing apparel, household goods, tools, implements to the value of $600. Certain other articles.	Householder or woman. Male person, not householder, has similar exemption ($450) not including household	Earnings of $85 or less per week are entirely exempt; and 90% of earnings for services within 60 days before

| State | Personal Property | | Wages |
	Amount	Who May Claim	
N.Y. (cont.)		furniture.	and any time after income execution: exemption may be reduced by amount court determines unnecessary for reasonable requirements of debtor and dependents.
North Carolina	$500 in property to be selected by owner.	Resident	Earnings for personal services for 60 days preceding levy if necessary for support of family.
North Dakota	Head of a family, money or personal property $2,000; single person, money or personal property, $150. All wearing apparel and clothing of the debtor and his family or one year's provisions and fuel and crops raised by him on an area not to exceed 160 acres occupied as his homestead.	Head of a family or single person.	Greater of 75% of debtor's disposable earnings or of excess of 40 times Federal minimum hourly wage rate. 100% of earnings for personal services within 60 days can be exempted by judge upon affidavit of need for support of family.
Ohio	Certain specified articles, including wearing apparel, tools and implements for carrying out profession, trade or business and a portion of personal earnings for services rendered within 30 days before the issuing of the attachment. The dollar amounts of these articles are greater in the case of a head of a family.	Resident.	75% of disposable earnings for week or excess of 30 times federal minimum hourly wage, whichever is greater.
Oklahoma	Numerous articles, household furniture, books, pictures, wearing apparel, specified animals, tools, etc.	Resident.	Resident homeowner and head of family – 75% of wages earned during last 90 days. Non-head of family – 75% of wages. Judgment arising from consumer debts: 75% of disposable earnings for workweek or amount equal to 30 times federal minimum wage, whichever is greater. Earnings 90 days before issuance of execution is 100% exempt if necessary for support of family. For judgments arising on debt resulting from consumer credit sale the greater of 75% of disposable earnings per workweek or amount each week equal to 30 times Federal minimum hourly wage.

State	Personal Property Amount	Who May Claim	Wages
Okla. (cont.)			No exemption for wages for any clerk, mechanic, laborer or servant. For family support orders — 100% exemption, but it does not apply to orders for child support.
Oregon	Books, pictures, musical instruments $75; wearing apparel $100 and for each member of the family $50; poultry $300; certain domestic animals, tools, library, etc., necessary in carrying on trade or profession, to $800 except for payment of debt contracted to assist in carrying on trade or profession; vehicle in the amount of $400 but vehicle plus property necessary to carry on trade or business may not exceed $800. No article is exempt from execution on a judgment recovered for its purchase price.	Householder.	Greater of 75% of disposable earnings for week or amount by which disposable earnings exceed 30 times the Federal minimum hourly wage.
Pennsylvania	$300 in real or personal property, also sewing machines, wearing apparel, other specified articles and certain leased articles.	Resident.	100% of all wages; does not apply to support orders.
Rhode Island	Wearing apparel, household goods to value of $1,000, tools used in trade to value of $500. Certain personal property of a housekeeper not exceeding $1,000.	Resident.	Not exceeding $50.
South Carolina	$500, not to apply on articles upon which judgment was obtained. Clothes, tools for trade, value $300. Partner entitled to exemption against individual creditors out of his partnership interest.	Head of family. Persons not head of family.	100% of earnings for personal services within 60 days before garnishment court order, if necessary for support of family. Judgments for fuel, food and medicine 15% of wages up to $100 excluded from general exemption at discretion of court.
South Dakota	$1,500 to head of family. $900 to person not head of family. Both of the above are in addition to what are known as absolute exemptions.	Debtor, his agent or attorney, head of family or in case of his failure to do so by any member of his family over the age of 14 years.	100% of earnings for personal services within 60 days if necessary for support of family.
Tennessee	Personal property up to $1,500 for head of household. Personal property up to	Both head and non-head of family who are bona fide citizens and permanent residents of	Wages to the extent of 50% or $20 per week whichever is greater, with a maximum total

| State | Personal Property | | Wages |
	Amount	Who May Claim	
Tenn. (cont.)	$900 for one not the head of a household.	Tennessee.	exemption of $50 per week. 40% or $17.50 per week whichever is greater, with a maximum total exemption of $40 per week, for a resident who is not the head of a family.
Texas	Personal property not to exceed an aggregate fair market value of $15,000 for each single adult person and $30,000 for a family which can include the following: furnishings of a home; all the following implements necessary for farming or ranching: tools, equipment, books used in trade or profession, wearing apparel, firearms, athletic and sporting equipment. Any two of the following means of travel: two animals, a saddle and bridle for each: horses, colts, mules, donkeys, bicycle or motorcycle, wagon, cart or dray, automobile, station wagon, truck trailer, camper truck, truck, pick-up truck; livestock and fowl not to exceed the following in number and forage on hand reasonably necessary for their consumption: five cows and their calves, one breeding age bull, 20 hogs, 20 sheep, 20 goats, 50 chickens, 30 turkeys, 30 ducks, 30 geese, 30 guineas; dog, cat and other household pets.	Every family.	Current wages.
Utah	Specified articles such as furniture up to $300 and tools or implements of trade to $500.	Head of family.	Married man or head of family one-half of earnings for 30 days prior to levy if head of family and his earnings are necessary for their support. Minimum exemption of $80 per month. Judgments arising from debts on consumer credit sales greater of 75% of disposable earnings per week or 40 times Federal minimum hourly wage.
Vermont	Specified articles. Specified professional books, clergyman, physician, dentist and lawyer, value $200.	Resident.	75% of disposable earnings for week or excess of 30 times Federal minimum hourly wage whichever is greater.

State	Personal Property Amount	Who May Claim	Wages
Virginia	Household goods, furniture and appliances of house-holder not to exceed $1,000. Many enumerated articles. Exemption not allowed against purchse price of article sought to be exempted or on shifting stocks of merchandise. A war veteran with 40% disability is entitled to an additional $1,000.	Resident householder or head of family.	75% of disposable earnings for that week or of excess of 30 times Federal minimum hourly wage, whichever is greater. Exemption is inapplicable to court order for support.
Washington	Household furniture and utensils, $1,000. $400 of other goods (no more than $100 in cash), wearing apparel, but not to exceed $500 in value of furs, jewelry and personal items. Many specially enumerated articles. Pension and life insurance also exempt.	Householder in case of household furniture. Beneficiary in case of pensions and life insurance.	The greater part of 40 times the state hourly minimum wage or of 75% of the disposable earnings of the defendant is exempt from garnishment. Disposable earnings means that part of the earnings remaining after deduction of the amounts required by law to be withheld.
West Virginia	$1,000 for husband, parent residing in state, infant children of deceased parents. Many special articles. $50 worth of tools or implements.	Resident and head of family only.	80% of wages due or to become due within one year after issuance of execution. $20 per week minimum.
Wisconsin	Automobiles used and kept for purpose of carrying on debtor's business to value of $1,000. Small tools and implements not exceeding $200 in value, and one tractor worth $1,500. Apparel not to exceed $400 and furniture up to $200.	Resident. Mechanic, artisan or laborer.	Greater of 75% of debtor's disposable earnings or of excess of 30 times Federal minimum hourly wage rate. Disposable earnings means that part of earnings after deduction of amounts required by law to be withheld. Employee with dependents — basic exemption of $120 plus $20 per dependent for each 30 day period prior to service of process, maximum exemption 75% of income. Employee without dependents — basic exemption of 60% of income for each 30 day period prior to service of process. Minimum $75, maximum $100.
Wyoming	Bible, pictures, school books, lot in cemetery, furniture, provisions, household articles, value $500, clothing value $150. Tools, teams, implements, stock in trade to carry on busi-	Head of family or person 60 years or over residing in state. Every resident. Professional men.	Judgments on consumer credit sales, home or loan; greater of 75% of disposable earnings or excess over 30 times Federal minimum wage. Otherwise, 50% of

State	Personal Property Amount	Who May Claim	Wages
Wyo. (cont.)	ness not over $300 and library, instruments and implements, $300.		earnings for personal services within 60 days before levy if necessary for use of resident family.

UNITED STATES DISTRICT COURT FOR THE

DISTRICT OF

In re

BANKRUPTCY NO.

Bankrupt

Include here all names used by bankrupt within last 6 years.

STATEMENT OF AFFAIRS
FOR BANKRUPT
ENGAGED IN BUSINESS

Each question should be answered or the failure to answer explained. If the answer is "none," this should be stated. If additional space is needed for the answer to any question, a separate sheet, properly identified, and made part hereof, should be used and attached.

If the bankrupt is a partnership or a corporation, the questions shall be deemed to be addressed to, and shall be answered on behalf of, the partnership or corporation; and the statement shall be verified by a member of the partnership or by a duly authorized officer of the corporation.

The term, "original petition," as used in the following questions, shall mean the petition filed under Bankruptcy Rule 103, 104, or 105.

1. Nature, location, and name of business.

a. Under what name and where do you carry on your business?

b. In what business are you engaged?
(If business operations have been terminated, give the date of such termination.)

c. When did you commence such business?

d. Where else, and under what other names, have you carried on business within the 6 years immediately preceding the filing of the original petition herein?
(Give street addresses, the name of any partners, joint adventurers, or other associates, the nature of the business, and the periods for which it was carried on.)

e. What is your employer identification number? Your social security number?

2. Books and records.

a. By whom, or under whose supervision, have your books of account and records been kept during the 2 years immediately preceding the filing of the original petition herein?
(Give names, addresses, and periods of time.)

b. By whom have your books of account and records been audited during the 2 years immediately preceding the filing of the original petition herein?
(Give names, addresses, and dates of audits.)

c. In whose possession are your books of account and records?
(Give names and addresses.)

d. If any of these books or records are not available, explain.

e. Have any books of account or records relating to your affairs been destroyed, lost, or otherwise disposed of within the 2 years immediately preceding the filing of the original petition herein?
(If so, give particulars, including date of destruction, loss, or disposition, and reason therefor.)

3. Financial statements.

Have you issued any written financial statements within the 2 years immediately preceding the filing of the original petition herein?
(Give dates, and the names and addresses of the persons to whom issued, including mercantile and trade agencies.)

4. Inventories.

a. When was the last inventory of your property taken?

b. By whom, or under whose supervision, was this inventory taken?

c. What was the amount, in dollars, of the inventory?
(State whether the inventory was taken at cost, market, or otherwise.)

d. When was the next prior inventory of your property taken?

e. By whom, or under whose supervision, was this inventory taken?

f. What was the amount, in dollars, of the inventory?
(State whether the inventory was taken at cost, market, or otherwise.)

g. In whose possession are the records of the 2 inventories above referred to?
(Give names and addresses.)

5. Income other than from operation of business.

What amount of income, other than from operation of your business, have you received during each of the 2 years immediately preceding the filing of the original petition herein?
(Give particulars, including each source, and the amount received therefrom.)

6. Tax returns and refunds.

a. In whose possession are copies of your federal and state income tax returns for the 3 years immediately preceding the filing of the original petition herein?

b. What tax refunds (income or other) have you received during the 2 years immediately preceding the filing of the original petition herein?

c. To what tax refunds (income or other), if any, are you, or may you be, entitled?
(Give particulars, including information as to any refund payable jointly to you and your spouse or any other person.)

7. Bank accounts and safe deposit boxes.

a. What bank accounts have you maintained, alone or together with any other person, and in your own or any other name, within the 2 years immediately preceding the filing of the original petition herein?
(Give the name and address of each bank, the name in which the deposit was maintained, and the name and address of every person authorized to make withdrawals from such account.)

b. What safe deposit box or boxes or other depository or depositories have you kept or used for your securities, cash, or other valuables within the 2 years immediately preceding the filing of the original petition herein?

(Give the name and address of the bank or other depository, the name in which each box or other depository was kept, the name and address of every person who had the right of access thereto, a description of the contents thereof, and, if the box has been surrendered, state when surrendered or, if transferred, when transferred and the name and address of the transferee.)

8. Property held for another person.

What property do you hold for any other person?
(Give name and address of each person, and describe the property, the amount or value thereof and all writings relating thereto.)

9. Prior bankruptcy proceedings.

What proceedings under the Bankruptcy Act have previously been brought by or against you?
(State the location of the bankruptcy court, the nature and number of proceeding, and whether a discharge was granted or refused, the proceeding was dismissed, or a composition arrangement, or plan was confirmed.)

10. Receiverships, general assignments, and other modes of liquidation.

a. Was any of your property, at the time of the filing of the original petition herein, in the hands of a receiver, trustee, or other liquidating agent?
(If so, give a brief description of the property and the name and address of the receiver, trustee, or other agent, and, if the agent was appointed in a court proceeding, the name and location of the court and the nature of the proceeding.)

b. Have you made any assignment of your property for the benefit of your creditors, or any general settlement with your creditors, within the 2 years immediately preceding the filing of the original petition herein?
(If so, give dates, the name and address of the assignee, and a brief statement of the terms of assignment or settlement.)

11. Property in hands of third person.

Is any other person holding anything of value in which you have an interest?
(Give name and address, location and description of the property, and circumstances of the holding.)

12. Suits, executions, and attachments.

a. Were you a party to any suit pending at the time of the filing of the original petition herein?
(If so, give the name and location of the court and the title and nature of the proceeding.)

b. Were you a party to any suit terminated within the year immediately preceding the filing of the original petition herein?
(If so, give the name and location of the court, the title and nature of the proceeding, and the result.)

c. Has any of your property been attached, garnished, or seized under any legal or equitable process within the 4 months immediately preceding the filing of the original petition herein?
(If so, describe the property seized or person garnished, and at whose suit.)

13. Payments on loans and installment purchases.

What repayments on loans in whole or in part, and what payments on installment purchases of goods and services, have you made during the year immediately preceding the filing of the original petition herein?
(Give the names and addresses of the persons receiving payment, the amounts of the loans and of the purchase price of the goods and services, the dates of the original transactions, the amounts and dates of payments, and, if any of the payees are your relatives, the relationship; if the bankrupt is a partnership and any of the payees is or was a partner or a relative of a partner, state the relationship; if the bankrupt is a corporation and any of the payees is or was an officer, director, or stockholder, or a relative of an officer, director, or stockholder, state the relationship.)

14. Transfers of property.

a. Have you made any gifts, other than ordinary and usual presents to family members and charitable donations, during the year immediately preceding the filing of the original petition herein?
(If so, give names and addresses of donees and dates, description, and value of gifts.)

b. Have you made any other transfer, absolute or for the purpose of security, or any other disposition which was not in the ordinary course of business during the year immediately preceding the filing of the original petition herein?
(Give a description of the property, the date of the transfer or disposition, to whom transferred or how disposed of, and state whether the transferee is a relative, partner, shareholder, officer, or director, the consideration, if any, received for the property, and the disposition of such consideration.)

15. Accounts and other receivables.

Have you assigned, either absolutely or as security, any of your accounts or other receivables during the year immediately preceding the filing of the original petition herein?
(If so, give names and addresses of assignees.)

16. Repossessions and returns.

Has any property been returned to, or repossessed by, the seller or by a secured party during the year immediately preceding the filing of the original petition herein?
(If so, give particulars, including the name and address of the party getting the property and its description and value.)

17. Business leases.

If you are a tenant of business property, what are the name and address of your landlord, the amount of your rental, the date to which rent had been paid at the time of the filing of the original petition herein, and the amount of security held by the landlord?

18. Losses.

a. Have you suffered any losses from fire, theft, or gambling during the year immediately preceding the filing of the original petition herein?
(If so, give particulars, including dates, names, and places, and the amounts of money or value and general description of property lost.)

b. Was the loss covered in whole or part by insurance?
(If so, give particulars.)

19. Withdrawals.

a. If you are an individual proprietor of your business, what personal withdrawals of any kind have you made from the business during the year immediately preceding the filing of the original petition herein?

b. If the bankrupt is a partnership or corporation, what withdrawals, in any form (including compensation or loans), have been made by any member of the partnership, or by any officer, director, managing executive, or shareholder of the corporation, during the year immediately preceding the filing of the original petition herein?
(Give the name and designation or relationship to the bankrupt of each person, the dates and amounts of withdrawals, and the nature or purpose thereof.)

20. Payments or transfers to attorneys.

a. Have you consulted an attorney during the year immediately preceding or since the filing of the original petition herein?
(Give date, name, and address.)

b. Have you during the year immediately preceding or since the filing of the original petition herein paid any money or transferred any property to the attorney, or to any other person on his behalf?
(If so, give particulars, including amount paid or value of property transferred and date of payment or transfer.)

c. Have you, either during the year immediately preceding or since the filing of the original petition herein, agreed to pay any money or transfer any property to an attorney at law, or to any other person on his behalf?
(If so, give particulars, including amount and terms of obligation.)

(If the bankrupt is a partnership or corporation, the following additional question should be answered.)

21. Members of partnership; officers, directors, managers, and principal stockholders of corporation.

a. What is the name and address of each member of the partnership, or the name, title, and address of each officer, director, and managing executive, and of each stockholder holding 25 per cent or more of the issued and outstanding stock, of the corporation?

b. During the year immediately preceding the filing of the original petition herein, has any member withdrawn from the partnership, or any officer, director, or managing executive of the corporation terminated his relationship, or any stockholder holding 25 per cent or more of the issued stock disposed of more than 50 per cent of his holdings?
(If so, give name and address and reason for withdrawal, termination, or disposition, if known.)

c. Has any person acquired or disposed of 25 per cent or more of the stock of the corporation during the year immediately preceding the filing of the petition?
(If so, give name and address and particulars.)

State of _____ County of _____ ss.:

I, _____ do hereby swear that I*

have read the answers contained in the foregoing statement of affairs and that they are true and complete to the best of my knowledge, information, and belief.

Subscribed and sworn to before me on

_____
Bankrupt

_____

_____
Official character

OF 8 statement of affairs: engaged in business: page 3   © 1973 by JULIUS BLUMBERG, INC.,

* Person verifying for partnership or corporation should indicate position or relationship to bankrupt.